Sous Vide Cookbook

Best Sous Vide Recipes for Perfectly Cooked Meals

Maxwell Parker

Sous Vide Cookbook

© Copyright 2020 Maxwell Parker All rights reserved.

Written by Maxwell Parker

First Edition

Copyrights Notice

Limited Liability

Please note that content of this book is based on personal experience and various information sources.

Although the author has made every effort to present accurate, up-to-date, reliable and complete information in this book, they make no representations or warranties with respect to the accuracy or completeness of the content of this book and specifically disclaim any implied warranties of merchantability or fitness for a particular purpose.

Your particular circumstances may not be suited to the example illustrated in this book; in fact, they likely will not be. You should use the information in this book at your own risk.

All trademarks, service marks, product names and the characteristics of any names mentioned in this book are considered the property of their respective owners and are used only for reference. No endorsement is implied when we use one of these terms.

This book is only for personal use. Please note the information contained within this document is for educational and entertainment purposes only and no warranties of any kind are declared or implied. Readers acknowledge that the author is not engaging in the rendering of legal, financial or professional advice.

Please consult a licensed professional before attempting any techniques outlined in this book. Nothing in this book is intended to replace common sense or legal accounting, or professional advice and is meant only to inform.

By reading this document, the reader agrees that under no circumstances is the author responsible for any losses, direct or indirect, which are incurred as a result of the use of information contained within this document, including, but not limited to, errors, omissions, or inaccuracies.

Table of Content

What do sous vide mean?

Sous-vide (French sous = under, vide = vacuum) or vacuum cooking is a unique cooking method in which the product to be prepared is the first vacuum-sealed in a unique plastic bag for subsequent cooking at low temperature in a water bath.

The cooking temperatures are below 100° C, which is why this method is particularly gentle: Due to the low heat, the products change more slowly at the molecular level, whereby the cooking result is all the more tender and juicy.

This method was invented by the French already in the 70s. Due to the lack of practical devices, however, vacuum cooking in private kitchens did not prevail until later.

Advantages of sous-vide cooking

In sous vide, the airtight packaging retains most of the flavors and nutrients, which is why vacuum-cooked foods are particularly aromatic. The preparation in a water bath achieves even better results than the already very gentle steam cooking. Beware of spices and herbs: These flavors intensify under vacuum. Therefore, use sparingly and season if necessary.

Unlike the preparation in the oven, in which the slow cooking is especially worthwhile for large pieces of meat, with the sous, vide method even smaller pieces can be cooked very well. Another advantage is that the core temperature is precisely controlled since the rule of thumb usually applies:

Water temperature = core temperature. An overcooking of the food is, therefore almost impossible at the right temperature, since the individual ingredients can at most assume the temperature of the water.

How Sous-Vide Works

During sous-vide cooking, vacuum-packed foods are slowly drawn in hot water. Since food is different, the water temperature is not always the same, but so-called cooking ranges are given to help in choosing the right temperature and cooking time. Basically, gitl as healthy cooking: The harder or more compact the product - such as root vegetables or legumes - the longer the cooking time. Fish and meat thus need shorter times than, for example, root vegetables and solid fruits.

Accessories are required for the sous vide cooking method:

- Unique vacuum bags or plastic bags that do not contain plasticizers or the like. can deliver to the food and are heat resistant
- Vacuum sealer
- Thermalizer: Hanging thermostat suspended in a pot filled with water to regulate the water temperature, or a compact water bath (sous-vide device) that also regulates the temperature automatically
- Food of the highest quality

Sous-vide step by step

- Prepare the product and season it sparingly
- Place it in the bag in portions, leaving at least 8 cm of space up to the opening for a smooth, tight weld when vacuuming
- Remove some air from the bag and make sure that the edges of the bag in the vacuum sealer are clean together to obtain a closed weld
- Put the bag with the vacuumed food in the water bath

Note: Make sure that the bag is entirely underwater for the entire cooking time. If necessary, complain

- Set the cooking time and the target temperature and if possible use a lid to heat more efficiently
- Carefully remove cooked products from the bag and serve or finish immediately (eg, roast)

Serving tips

Products that cook in the pan can be browned outside and dry on the inside, but still raw and juicy, because the core temperature is lower. These different cooking levels are not possible with the sous vide, because the product pulls evenly. So if you miss the browned crust and the roasted flavors of the meat, fry it shortly after the water bath in the pan. The roast incidentally also reduces the risk of bacteria, and the meat is then hot enough to serve it. But be careful: Roast the meat only very briefly, otherwise the sous vide effect disappears, and the meat gets dry.

Store vacuumed food

Without direct air contact, vacuumed food can be stored or frozen for longer if it is suitable. With prepared sous-vide products, the condition is that an abrupt cooling takes place after cooking. Otherwise, germs and bacteria can multiply due to the low temperatures. Place the bags in ice water, which should never exceed 5 ° C.

Practical: If you expect guests, you can cook your meals days in advance and reheat the vacuumed food before you eat it. Taste and appearance suffer by no means.

Here are the Sous Vide Recipes

Beef steak sous vide with red wine reduction

Ingredients For 2:

- Portions
- 2 Beef steak (s) (hip steak), approx. 250 g each
- 4 branch / s rosemary
- 4 branch / s thyme
- 100 ml port wine
- 150 ml red wine
- Olive oil, good
- Clarified butter
- Sea salt, coarse
- Pepper (steak pepper)
- 1 teaspoon, heaped   sugar
- 1 tbsp   Butter, cold

Preparation:

- Working time approx. 20 min.
- Cooking / baking time approx. 100 min.
- Total time approx. 120 min.

Dab the beef steaks dry and vacuum one at a time with a sprig of thyme and rosemary, and a small dash of olive oil. Heat the Sous Vide bath to 56 degrees and then put the bags in it.

Before the end of the cooking time, caramelise the sugar in a saucepan and deglaze with the red wine and the port. Add the remaining herbs and simmer the wine gently.

Take the steaks out of the water bath after 90 minutes. Set up a pan with buttered lard and let the butter get really hot. In the meantime dab the steaks lightly. Sauté the steaks in the butter briefly for about 5 to 10 seconds from each side, then wrap in aluminum foil and keep warm.

Add the wine mixture to the pan and reduce to 1/3, season to taste with salt and pepper and simmer with a little butter. Put the sauce on the plate and put the steak on top, sprinkle with the coarse salt and pepper. This is very well with baked potatoes.

Pork rag sous vide

From the Mangalitza pig 20 min.

Ingredients for 4 portions:

- 800 g Pork, (Mangalitza or organic pig's back)
- 2 toe / n garlic
- 3 tbsp butter
- 1 Bay leaf
- Olive oil

- Pepper, black from the mill
- Salt

Preparation:

- Working time approx. 20 min.
- Resting time approx . 120 min.
- Total time approx. 140 min.

Rub in the back piece with a little olive oil and cover with garlic slices and the bay leaf and vacuum.

Place in a 60 ° warm water bath for approx. 75 - 90 minutes. Alternatively, it is also in the steamer. Time is of minor importance as the meat cannot get warmer than 60 °. I'd rather let it stay longer if you're unsure.

Then take out the pork, froth the butter in a hot pan and fry the meat in it for a short time. Season it with salt and pepper and cut up. It goes well with risotto and roasted vegetables (eg pointed pepper). The meat is then superzart, slightly pink and very tasty.

Carpaccio of pork fillet - Sous Vide cooked

Cook sous vide in the oven

Ingredients For 4:

- Portions
- 1 Pork (s)
- 1 bunch arugula
- 1 some cherry tomatoes
- 1 Lemons)
- Parmesan, (shavings planed)
- Olive oil, extra virgin
- 2 bay leaves
- 2 Garlic cloves)
- Salt
- Pepper

Preparation:

- Working time approx. 30 min.
- Cooking / baking time approx. 90 min.
- Total time approx. 120 min.

Brush the washed and carefully parsley pork tenderloin with olive oil, season with salt and pepper, then sauté with the bay leaves and the sliced garlic cloves. Cook in a water bath at 60 ° for 90 minutes.

Cut the chopped filet into thin slices and arrange on plates. Season with salt and pepper from the mill, spread the rocket and the quartered tomatoes on the meat, drizzle with lemon juice and a little olive oil and sprinkle with the chips of Parmesan cheese.

Do not own a Sous Vide-Garer, but use the oven and a cast-iron roaster without lid. However, a wireless roasting thermometer is indispensable for this. Heat the water in the roasting pan on the stove to the desired temperature and off in the preheated oven. Constant monitoring of the temperature and possibly low readjustment allow me a constant water temperature +/- 1 °. The temperature setting of the oven should be tested beforehand.

Pea rice

Ingredients:

- 1 cup   Brown rice, z. B. Basmati, round grain or wild rice
- 1 cup   water
- 1 cup   Peas, TK
- vegetable stock
- pepper
- garlic powder
- turmeric
- Salt or soy sauce (shoyu)

Working time:

- approx. 2 minutes
- Cooking / baking time: approx. 22 minutes

Preparation:

Cook the brown rice with the spices for 1 hour in the water bath. In a different bag, put in the frozen peas, and when it's done, add salt or soy sauce to the plate.

Mango with Stick **y Rice**

Ingredients

- 200g sticky rice
- 400ml water
- 500ml Coconut milk, do not shake
- 45g sugar
- 10g salt
- 5g food starch
- 2 Mango (s), mature
- Sesame to the sprinkling

Cooking / baking time:

- approx. 2 hours

Preparation:

1. Soak the rice inside water for at least one hour and then rinse.
2. Pour the rice into bag and then place inside water bath. Meanwhile, open the coconut milk and spoon the thick

coconut cream floating on top into a small bowl. This corresponds approximately to the upper quarter of the pack.

3. Place the remaining light coconut milk in a small pan and heat it with two-thirds of the sugar, equivalent to about 2 tablespoons, and heat 3/4 of the salt over a medium flame for 5 minutes, but do not boil.

4. At the end of the cooking, drain the steam from the water bath and pour the rice from the bag into a bowl and gradually stir in the boiled coconut milk and let it steep for 15 minutes.

5. Put the coconut cream in the empty pan, add the remaining third of the sugar, about 1 tablespoon and the remaining salt and bring to a boil. Mix the cornstarch and a bit of cold water and add, the coconut mixture is thickened a bit.

6. Cut a small piece of mango at the bottom so you can put it up. Peel the mangoes, cut the slices and cut into small pieces.

7. To serve, place the rice mixture in a small bowl, sprinkle the mango pieces next to it, drizzle over the thick coconut mixture and decorate the dessert with sesame seeds.

Beef with ajada

This chard with ajada is a classic of simple family cuisine. A good fresh product and a quality paprika are the secrets of the court.

Ingredients for 2 persons:

- 300g of fresh chard leaves (Pencas are reserved for another bowl)
- 1 big potato
- 3 garlic cloves
- 1 teaspoon of La Vera paprika
- Extra virgin olive oil
- Salt and pepper

Preparation:

1. Peel off the potatoes and then cut rather thickly. We wash well and smell the leaves of thick chard. You can use chilled packs of freshly cut, welded chard leaves.
2. You need vegetables, cakes and potatoes together for about 30 minutes until the potatoes are tender, but whole. You can stew it or in very little salt water. Wash it in the fire and only with water to wash the vegetables so as not to lose any of its properties.
3. Peel garlic and filetamos. We brown them in the fire in a little olive oil, and when they take on the color, we take them out of the fire and put down the peppers. We stir until the sauce is mixed, and we water the vegetables when it is served, very hot.
4. This recipe can also be made with vegetables such as green beans, spinach or cabbage. The preparatory process is the same.
5. Part of this can be done using the water bath.

Greek salad

This Greek salad recipe has the best Mediterranean flavors: cheese, tomatoes, olives. If you can not find the Greek olives of Kalamata, use black olives.

Ingredients for 2 persons:

150 g fat

- 1 tomato salad or a handful of cherry tomatoes
- Mixed salad
- cucumber
- Optional: 1 small yellow pepper or red (or both)
- purple onion or fresh green to taste
- 50 g black olives (in the original recipe are Kalamata olives)
- Olive oil, with white wine vinegar, salt and pepper
- 1 teaspoon oregano

The preparations:

1. Wash the vegetables well. Slice the tomatoes, onions and peppers or cut them to taste and cut the cucumbers into thin slices.
2. Place in a salad bowl a bag, with the salad well washed and well aerated (or better centrifuged), seal it with the mixture of ingredients and garnish with chopped cheese.

3. Prepare the vinaigrette in a separate bag with three parts of oil for a vinegar (if you want more, use balsamic vinegar), salt and pepper too. Mix the vinaigrette well until it is very dense, almost emulsified as mayonnaise. Pour this sauce on the salad. Sprinkle with oregano if you want and serve it cold and immediately.
4. If you do not want to serve it right now, hold on to the bandage and finally put it on when serving it so it will not deteriorate.

Mediterranean salad

This Mediterranean salad is light but with an intense flavor and a garlic vinaigrette for the bravest. If you want, you can season with a traditional vinaigrette.

Ingredients for 2 persons:

- 100 g different lettuce leaves
- 6 sun-dried tomatoes (store the oil for vinaigrette when stored)
- A handful of black olives
- 1 small box of anchovies with oil
- 75 g of feta, mozzarella or cream cheese of your choice

- Some basil leaves
- A handful of kidnappers
- For vinaigrette: extra virgin olive oil, white wine vinegar, a dash of garlic or half a teaspoon of garlic and salt powder

The preparations:

1. We have the washed salad in a bowl or a serving tray and we dispose of the rest of the ingredients in an orderly manner.
2. For the preparation of vinaigrette we use anchovy oil and the oil that dried tomato pots usually bring. We mix well and add extra virgin olive oil if needed.
3. We incorporate vinegar and salt (we need to be careful, as the anchovies and their oil already provide plenty of salt). We crush garlic, close small basil leaves (we all reserve) and also crush garlic.
4. We mix everything and season the salad when it is served.

Tortellini salad

Ingredients:

- Tortellini stuffed with cheese (better if it's fresh pasta)

- cherry tomatoes
- Basil leaves or fresh oregano
- coarse grated cheese (optional)
- Slices of green or black olives
- Sliced peppers
- Extra virgin olive oil
- a handful of kidnappers
- Sherry vinegar and salt

The preparations:

1. You must prepare the tortellini with a piece of oil and salt as per instructions in the container and allow to cool until they reach room temperature (they have more flavor than if they are cold in the fridge).
2. Cut the cherry tomatoes in half. Tortellini with tomatoes and chopped basil leaves or fresh oregano (here oregano) mix and sprinkle with grated cheese to emphasize the taste. Garnish with plenty of extra virgin olive oil, sherry vinegar and salt.

Egg cutter

Ingredients:

- 6 servings
- 6 eggs
- 6 slices of bacon or 6 bacon rolls
- Ham, optional
- Roasted cheese (white or American cheddar or mozzarella)
- Oregano or other aromatic herb (knife tip)
- salt and pepper
- Prisco Spray
- Cupcake mold
- Garlic-onion powder (knife tip)

The steps:

1. 2 to 3 hours
2. Inside the special bag, Lubricate the mold with the Crisco spray Or with oil.
3. Collect the basket of bacon. It has to cover most of the cupcakes in the form of a bowl. The other ingredients are resting. If you want, you can add ham, but do not forget to leave room for the other ingredients.
4. Put some grated cheese.
5. Add an egg, add onion and garlic powder (spread), add salt, pepper and oregano.
6. Add grated cheese covering the surface.
7. Put in water bath. Always cook the cheese so that it does not burn or spill. Approximately 15 minutes
8. To separate, you may need a small spoon to dislodge the suction cups from the mold.
9. Enjoy

Vegetable salad

Ingredients:

- 1/2 pound of frozen green beans
- 15 artichoke hearts (drained and chopped)
- 1 bunch of herbs (mixed, chopped)
- 2 red onions (peeled and sliced)
- 10 cherry tomatoes (divided into four parts)
- 2 1/2 oz black olives
- 6 tablespoons balsamic vinegar (light)
- 6 tablespoons olive oil

Preparation:

1. Blanch beans in boiling salted water, simmer for 30 mins, drain and rinse in cold water.
2. Mix vinegar, the oil and season to taste. Cover with vegetables and leave to marinate for 10 minutes before serving.

Tuna and vegetable salad

Ingredients:

- 2 medium-sized zucchini (thinly cut)
- 2 medium sized carrots (cut in matches)
- 3 cans of tuna (each 5 ounces drained in water)
- 4 sticks of celery (cut and chopped)
- 1 onion (small, thinly sliced)
- 1 tablespoon of fresh, flat parsley (chopped roughly)
- 4 lettuce leaves (iceberg)
- 1/2 cup dressing (light fench)
- 2 tablespoons of yogurt
- 1 garlic clove (crushed)
- 2 teaspoons curry powder

Preparation:

1. Cook the zucchini and carrots in water bath for 10 minute. Drain and change to cold water.
2. For dressing, add all the ingredients in a small bowl and season to taste.

3. Place the zucchini and carrots with tuna, celery, onions, parsley and dressing in a medium bowl and mix gently.
4. Add the salad to the lettuce leaves and serve.

Potato and vegetable salad with herb dressing

Ingredients:

- 1 pound of small potatoes (peeled and halved)
- 1/2 pound of green beans (cut and cut into pieces)
- 1 cauliflower (small, cut into florets)
- 1 main salad (torn into bite-sized pieces)
- 1 red pepper (without seeds and roughly chopped)
- 1 2/3 cups of yogurt
- 3 tablespoons mayonnaise
- 2 teaspoons of basil (mince, extra leaves for garnish)
- 2 teaspoons chives (finely chopped)
- 2 teaspoons parsley (finely chopped)

Preparation:

1. Boil the potatoes with little salt inside water bath for 50 minutes, until ready. Drain, cool and cut.

2. Boil the beans and the cauliflower florets inside boiling salted water for 7-8 minutes, till it's soft. Drain, rinse in cold water and allow cooling completely.
3. Put the cooled potatoes with beans and cauliflower in a bowl. Add salad and pepper and mix.
4. For the dressing: put the yoghurt and mayonnaise in a bowl, add the chopped herbs, season to taste and mix freshly ground black pepper.
5. Dress over the salad, garnish with the extra basil leaves and serve.

Raw root vegetable salad

Ingredient:

- 1/4 cup extra virgin olive oil
- 1 tablespoon of toasted sesame oil (use cold pressed olive oil for Passover)
- 1 tablespoon soy sauce (Passover soy sauce for passover use)
- 2 teaspoons of honey
- Grated peel and juice of 1 lime
- 1 teaspoon of well grated fresh ginger or 1 pinch of soil
- 1 carrot, peeled

- 1 onion fennel, cut
- 3 radishes, trimmed
- 1 medium-sized turnip, peeled
- 1 medium beetroot, peeled
- 2 tablespoons coarsely chopped hazelnuts
- 2 tablespoons of coarsely cut pistachios
- Freshly ground black pepper

Directions:

1. Prepare Dressing: Mix oil, soy sauce, honey, lime zest and juice and ginger in a large bowl. Put 2 tablespoons of the dressing into a small bowl and then set aside both bowls.
2. Cut carrot, fennel, radish and turnips into mandolin. Add to the bowl and then toss with the dressing. Cut the red beet into thin slices on the mandolin and scoop it into the small bowl with the dressing.
3. Put the beetroot slices in a bowl or divide them between the plates. Top with the remaining vegetables.
4. Put each preparation inside separate vacuum-sealable bags and then pour the stock mixture into the bags, dividing it evenly.
5. Season with the chopped nuts and pepper and serve.

Meatloaf

2 portions

Ingredients:

- 2 Shallot (s), peeled and finely diced
- 1 small one   Carrot (s), finely diced
- Beetroot, finely diced
- Parsley root (s), finely diced
- 2 tbsp olive oil
- 300 g minced meat
- (S) Egg
- 2 tbsp Panko
- 1 tbsp Dijon mustard
- 1 teaspoon Paprika powder, sweet or bar hat seasoning
- 1 small one Chili pepper (s), finely chopped
- 1 pinchSea salt and pepper from the mill
- 50 g Feta cheese, finely diced
- 1 bunch Chervil, chopped

Preparation

Working time: approx. 20 min.

Cooking time: approx. 35 min.

1. Sweat the shallots together with the diced vegetables in olive oil and allow to lightly color. Turn to the side to cool.
2. Mix minced meat with the egg, the mustard, the paprika powder or Baharat spice and the panco flour. If necessary, add the chili pepper.
3. Add the vegetables together and the feta cheese and the chopped chervil and mix well again and season with salt and pepper.
4. Place everything in a greased form into the Quick Clean Basket, close it and set the sous vide immersion circulator for use according to the manufacturer's instructions..
5. Cook it for about 50 minutes.
6. If you want to give the roast even a little whistle, you can wrap it from the outside with wafer-thin bacon slices.

Nutritional Information

- Saturated Fat 6.4g grams
- Trans Fat 0.7g grams
- 5%Total Carbohydrates 14g grams
- 5% Dietary Fiber 1.2g grams
- Sugars 6.1g grams
- Protein 27g

Cod with Nori algen Crust with Asian Vegetables from the Air fryer

Ingredients:

- 300 g Cod fillet (s), fresh, in good quality
- 1 / 2 tsp Peppercorns, white
- 1 / 2 tsp coriander seeds
- 2 Nori sheets
- 10 g butter
- Egg white, beaten half-solid
- Lemon (s), the abrasion of it
- 50 g Panko
- 80 g Sugar sheet (s), blanched and cut into strips
- 80 g Chicory, without stem, as whole leaf
- Spring onions, cut into rings
- Chili pepper (s), mild, cut into rings
- 3 tbsp coconut oil
- 3 tbsp Coconut blossom sugar
- Lemon (s), the juice and the shell of it
- 1 pinchSea salt and pepper from the mill
- 4 tbsp teriyaki sauce
- 1 branch / s Lemon balm or Thai basil
- 50 g Cashews, roasted

Preparation:

1. Wash the cod and pat dry.
2. Finely chop the nori leaves together with the peppercorns and the coriander seeds in a chopper and then mix well with the butter, the egg whites and the lemon.
3. Now add the pancake flour and process to a flaky mass. Evenly press the mixture evenly on the meat side of the cod.
4. Heat the coconut oil and caramelize the coconut sugar with the curry powder for a short time. Add the sliced vegetables and deglaze with lemon juice. Add some poultry stock and season with sea salt.
5. Swirl those vegetables inside a sauté use sous vide immersion circulator for use according to the manufacturer's directions until the desired bite is reached. Add the plucked herbs
6. Cook the cod on the skin side with another vacuum-sealable bags and pour the mixture into the bags on a greased at 180 ° C for 15 min
7. Finally, drizzle everything with a little Teriyaki sauce and drop wise sesame oil.

Nutritional Information:

- Saturated Fat 6.4g grams
- Trans Fat 0.7g grams
- Polyunsaturated Fat 1g grams
- Monounsaturated Fat 8.3g grams
- 41%Cholesterol 123mg milligrams
- 35%Sodium 844mg milligrams
- 5%Total Carbohydrates 14g grams
- 5% Dietary Fiber 1.2g grams
- Sugars 6.1g grams
- Protein 27g

The Classic Bacon with Eggs

Ingredients:

- 8 eggs
- 150 g bacon, sliced
- Cherry tomato (optional)
- Fresh parsley (optional)

Preparation:

1. Fry the eggs in the bacon fat the way you like. Cut the cherry tomatoes in half and cook into vacuum-sealable bags and pour Salt and pepper to taste.

Advice!

If you can, try using organic bacon, it's healthier and contains fewer additives.

Nutritional Information:

- Calories 236
- Calories from Fat 153 (64.8%)
- % Daily Value
- Total Fat 17g
- Saturated fat 6g
- Cholesterol 422mg

- Sodium 510mg   22%
- Carbohydrates 1g
- Net carbs 1g
- Fiber 0g 0%
- Glucose 1g
- Protein 19g

Greek Salad Pan Recipe

Time: 25 minutes

Ingredients :

(For 4 people)

- 8 eggs
- 1 spring onion
- 120 g of cherry tomatoes
- 100 g of black olives
- 100 g of feta cheese
- olive oil, salt
- chopped parsley

Preparation:

2. We will start beating the eggs with a pinch of salt and a spoonful of chopped parsley.

3. Chop the small onion and then place a nonstick skillet on the heat and add a drizzle of olive oil, sauté the onion for four minutes until it begins to be golden brown.

4. Add the halved cherry tomatoes and the black olives and cook for another two minutes until the tomatoes start to look soft inside vacuum-sealable bags and pour the mixture into the bags.

5. In a separate bag, add the beaten eggs, cook until we see the eggs set.

6. Add the crumbled feta cheese on top and grill for five minutes until we see the golden surface. Sprinkle with a little more fresh parsley.

Nutritional information:

- Calorie Goal1, 850 cal. 150 / 2,000 Cal left.
- Fat54g. 13 / 67gleft.
- Sodium 2,300g. 0 / 2,300gleft.
- Cholesterol 300g. 0 / 300gleft.

Broccoli with Chicken and Soy Sauce

Preparation:

Preparation: 10 min

Cooking: 10 min

Total: 20 min

Ingredients:

- 250 g broccoli
- 150 g onion
- 20 g cashew
- 1 breast (s) chicken
- For the sauce:
- 2 teaspoon garlic powder
- 1 teaspoon ginger powder
- 2 teaspoon (s) onion powder
- 2 tablespoon (s) vinegar of rice or another type of vinegar
- 2 tablespoon (s) soy sauce
- 1 tablespoon (s) sesame oil (can also be olive oil)

Preparation:

1. Place into vacuum-sealable bags and pour the mixture into the bags,
2. Prepare the sous vide immersion circulator for use according to the instructions. Put the bags inside the circulating water and then cook it for 30 minutes for medium doneness.
3. Remove the bags from the circulating water. Remove it from the bags and pat dry.

Nutritional information:

- Calories 376 Calories from fats 135
- Total fat 15g 23%
- Saturated fats 2g 10%

- Cholesterol 80mg 27%
- Sodium 1199mg 50%
- Potassium 1188mg 34%
- Total carbohydrates 26g 9%
- Fiber 5g 20%
- Sugars 8g
- Protein 35g 70%
- Vitamin A 16.3%
- Vitamin C 148.2%
- Calcium 9.5%
- Iron 16.6%

Shrimp & Sausage Skillet Dinner

Total Time: 5 mins

Servings: 4

Calories: 330 kcal

Ingredients:

- 1/4 cup of avocado oil divided

- 1 pound of shrimp peeled and deveined
- 1 tsp of Cajun Seasoning or Old Bay seasoning
- 12 ounces of chicken sausage cut into 1/2 inch slices
- 1 jalapeno minced
- 1 clove of garlic minced
- 1/2 lb of green beans cut into 2 inch pieces
- 1 medium size of red pepper cut into 2 inch slices
- Salt and pepper

Preparation:

1. Place into vacuum-sealable bags and pour the mixture into the bags,
2. Prepare sous vide immersion circulator for use according to the manufacturer's directions. Put the bags inside the circulating water and then cook.
3. Remove the bags from the circulating water. Remove it from the bags and pat dry. Serve it!

Nutrition Information:

- Shrimp & Sausage Skillet Dinner
- Amount Per Serving   (1 /4 of skillet)
- Calories 330 Calories from Fat 203
- % Daily Value
- Total Fat 22.51g 35%
- Total Carbohydrates 7.35g 2%
- Dietary Fiber 2.31g 9%
- Protein 31.85g 64%

Keto Shrimp Scampi

Prep Time: 5 mins

Cook Time: 10 mins

Total Time: 15 mins

Servings: 4

Ingredients:

- 4 tablespoons of butter
- 1 tablespoon of lemon juice
- 1 tablespoon of minced garlic
- 2 teaspoons of red pepper flakes
- 1 tablespoon of chopped chives or 1 teaspoon dried chives
- 1 tablespoon of minced basil leaves plus more for sprinkling or 1 teaspoon dried basil
- 2 tablespoons of chicken stock (or white wine)
- 1 lb of defrosted shrimp (21-25 count)

Preparation:

1. Place into vacuum-sealable bags and pour the mixture into the bags,

2. Prepare sous vide immersion circulator for use according to the manufacturer's directions. Preheat the water at126°F (52°C).
3. Put the bags inside the circulating water and cook for 30 minutes for medium doneness.
4. Remove the bags from the circulating water. Remove it from the bags and pat dry.
5. Stir at the end of the minute. The shrimp should be well-cooked at this point.
6. Sprinkle it with additional fresh basil leaves and then enjoy it.

Nutrition Information:

- 221kcal
- Fat: 13g
- Saturated fat: 7g
- Carbohydrates: 1g
- Protein: 23g

Office Recipes

Cooking time: 15 to 30 min

Ingredients:

- Servings: 2
- 4 slices of toast
- 120 g of ham
- 100 g pineapple (diced)
- Butter (for brushing)
- Salt
- Pepper
- 100 g of cheese

Preparation:

1. Place into vacuum-sealable bags and pour the mixture into the bags,
2. Prepare sous vide immersion circulator for use according to the manufacturer's directions. Preheat the water at126°F (52°C).
3. Put the bags inside the circulating water and cook for 30 minutes for medium doneness.
4. Remove the bags from the circulating water. Remove it from the bags and pat dry.
5. Stir at the end of the minute. The shrimp should be well-cooked at this point.
6. Sprinkle additional fresh basil leaves and enjoy.

Tip: Of course you can also use pineapple slices for the Toast Hawaii from the hot air fryer.

Nutrition Information:

- Calories 120
- % Daily Value
- 5%Total Fat 3g grams
- 8% Saturated Fat 1.5g grams

- Trans Fat 0g grams
- 7%Cholesterol 20mg milligrams
- 5%Sodium 125mg milligrams
- 7%Total Carbohydrates 22g grams
- 2% Dietary Fiber 0.5g grams
- Sugars 7g grams
- Protein 3g grams
- 0% Vitamin A
- 0% Vitamin C
- 0% Calcium
- 6% Iron

Beef Dish with Bird Lettuce

Cooking time: More than 60 min

Ingredients:

- Servings: 4
- 600 g boiled beef (cooked)
- 6 cl of Sherry Dry

- 2 carrots
- 2 turnips (yellow)
- 1/4 celeriac
- 4 tablespoons of chives (chopped)
- 600 ml of beef soup
- 10 sheets of gelatin
- Vegetable oil (for the form)
- Pepper (from the mill)
- Salt
- 200 g of bird's lettuce
- Pumpkinseed-pesto
- Chives (to sprinkle)

For The Marinade:

- 4 tablespoons of corn oil
- 3 tablespoons apple cider vinegar
- 2 tablespoons of beef soup
- Pinch of salt

Preparation:

1. Boil the soup with 200 ml of water.
2. Add carrots, yellow turnips and celery and cook until soft. Remove from the soup, let cool and cut into 3 mm thick strips.
3. Soak the gelatin in cold water, squeeze and add to the soup. Season well with sherry, salt and pepper and remove from Air fryer heat.
4. Spread the terrine mold with little oil, insert the plastic wrap lengthwise and smooth with kitchen paper.
5. Cut the top of the heated beef from the vaccum into 2 mm thick slices, dip each slice into the still warm soup one at a time and line the shape with it. In doing so, arrange overlapping about 6 cm over the edge.

6. Pour in a little soup, sprinkle with chives, place the vegetable strips lengthways and top them dipped in soup. Repeat this process three times; Pour in the rest of the soup.
7. Press foil and then try to refrigerate for 3 hours. For the marinade, mix all of the ingredients with a whisk and marinate the lettuce. Toss the terrine, remove the foil and cut into slices.
8. Arrange on chilled plates and garnish with the marinated lettuce. Drizzle with pumpkin seed pesto and sprinkle with chives.

Tip:

Depending on the season, the vegetable inlay of the Sulz can be modified with radishes, asparagus or pickled mushrooms. Drizzled with apple cider vinegar and sprinkled with Fleur de sel and pepper, the Sulz tastes even spicier.

Nutrition Information:

- 221kcal
- Fat: 13g
- Saturated fat: 7g
- Carbohydrates: 1g
- Protein: 23g

Beef Roulade with Pumpkin

Cooking time: More than 60 min

Ingredients:

- 4 pieces of beef schnitzel (approx. 170g each)
- 160 g pumpkin
- 8 slices of vulcano ham (or bacon)
- 60 g pickled gherkin
- 40 ml of oil
- 1.5 tablespoons of flour
- 100 g onion cubes
- 2 toes of garlic
- 100 ml cream
- 700 ml of beef soup
- Salt
- Pepper (from the mill)
- 1 tbsp estrone mustard
- Some flour (for dusting)

Preparation:

1. Tap the slices thinly, if necessary, cut the edges, salt and pepper. Brush the surface with mustard and put on bacon slices.
2. Cut the pumpkin into thin pieces and place with the gherkins on the edge of the roulades. Roll up the roulades, fix with metal skewers, toothpicks, clamps or splits.
3. Turn the roulades into flour, prepare the vaccum, and cook the roulades on all sides and then remove.
4. Roast the onion lightly, add the flour and roast briefly. Add soup and immediately stir with the whisk until the flour lumps dissolve.
5. Put in the roulades and steam about 1.5 hours.
6. Remove roulades from the sauce and keep warm.
7. Pass the sauce, add the cream and cook again. Then spicy taste. If necessary, thicken with a little touch of starch.
8. Remove roulades from the spaghetti or needles, arrange on plates and douse with the sauce.
9. These include noodles, mashed potatoes.

Nutritional Information:

- Calories 135 Calories from Fat 22.5.
- Total Fat 2.5 g 4%
- Saturated Fat 1.2 g 6%
- Unsaturated Fat 0.3 g.
- Cholesterol 2.7 mg 1%
- Sodium 205.4 mg 9%
- Total Carbohydrate 25.4 g 8%
- Dietary Fiber 3.5 g 14%

Liver with Onion and Apple Slices

Cooking time: 15 to 30 min

Ingredients:

- Portions: 3
- 1 piece of pork liver (or calf's liver, approx. 350g)
- 3-4 pieces of shallots (or onions)
- 3-4 pieces of apples
- 2 teaspoons sugar
- 1/8 l white wine
- 2 - 3 teaspoon soup spices (powder)
- Kren (at will)

Preparation:

1. For the liver with onion and apple slices, cut the shallots or onions into large cubes, sauté in a pan with a little fat. Deglaze with the white wine and reduce. Add the soup powder and a little whine, add sugar to taste.
2. Cook for few minutes with the vacuum-sealable bags. Season with salt and pepper. Place the liver in a casserole dish, cover with the shallot-apple cube mixture and heat the liver with onion and apple slices for about 20 minutes.

Tip:

The liver tastes particularly good with onion and apple slices, if you serve a homemade mashed potato.

Nutrition Information:

- Shrimp & Sausage Skillet Dinner
- Amount Per Serving   (1 /4 of skillet)
- Calories 330 Calories from Fat 203
- % Daily Value
- Total Fat 22.51g 35%
- Total Carbohydrates 7.35g 2%
- Dietary Fiber 2.31g 9%
- Protein

Asparagus vegetables

Cooking time: 15 to 30 min

Ingredients:

Servings: 2

- 4 bars of asparagus (white)
- 4 bars of asparagus (green)
- 1 tbsp butter
- 1 pinch of salt

- pepper
- sugar
- 2 pcs. Paradeiser (gutted, diced)
- 100 ml of soup
- 2 sprigs of lemon balm (leaves peeled, chopped)

Preparation:

1. For the asparagus Wash the asparagus, peel, remove ends, cut into small pieces and mix with the butter, 1 pinch of salt, pepper and sugar.
2. Core the Paradeiser and cut into fine cubes.
3. Add the asparagus to the baking tray add the soup and heat at 160 ° C in the vacuum-sealable bags.
4. After about 12-15 minutes add the dice and cook for another 5 minutes.
5. Then remove the asparagus and stir chopped lemon balm under the finished asparagus.

Grenadier Pancakes with Fried Egg

Cooking time: 30 to 60 min

Ingredients:

Servings: 2

- 200 g potatoes (cooked the day before)
- 150 g noodles (cooked, or, if available, dumpling leftovers)
- 250 g leek
- 50 g bacon
- 50 grams of cured meat
- 1/2 piece of onion (white, peeled)
- 1-2 toes of garlic (peeled)
- 15 g of butter
- 2 eggs
- 1 KL marjoram (dried)
- 1 KL caraway (ground)
- salt
- Pepper (from the mill)
- 1/2 bunch chives

Preparation:

1. For Grenadier schmarrn with fried egg bacon and cut into strips or cubes. Dice the onion and garlic, wash the leek, dry and cut into fine rings.
2. Cut the potatoes into 2 x 2 cm cubes and cook with some butter vacuum-sealable bags for 30mins. Add remaining ingredients, except the eggs, to the potatoes and then mix well.
3. Finish stirring for an additional 20 minutes at 170 ° C with occasional stirring. Fry the fried eggs and serve the grenadier pancakes garnished with fried eggs and freshly cut chives.

Tip:

Grenadier pancakes with fried egg is a great leftover and can be varied or supplemented with other ingredients.

Nutritional Information:

- Total Fat 10 g 15%

- Saturated fat 2.1g 10%
- Polyunsaturated fat 4.4 g
- Monounsaturated fat 2.5 g
- Cholesterol 59 mg 19%
- Sodium 439 mg 18%
- Potassium 132 mg 3%
- Total Carbohydrate 28 g 9%
- Protein 6 g 12%

Savory Chicken Thighs with Grill Marinade

Cooking time: 30 to 60 min

Ingredients:

Servings: 4

- 1 toe garlic (crushed)
- 1/2 tablespoon mustard
- 2 tsp sugar (brown)
- 1 teaspoon chilli powder
- Pepper (black, freshly ground)

- 1 tbsp olive oil
- 5 pcs chicken lower leg

Preparation:

1. For the spicy chicken legs with grill marinade, mix the garlic with the mustard, the brown sugar, the chili powder, a pinch of salt and freshly ground pepper. Mix with the oil.
2. Rub in the chicken thighs with the marinade and marinate for 20 minutes.
3. Put the chicken thighs into vacuum-sealable bags.
4. Cook the chicken thighs at 200 ° C until brown. Then reduce the temperature to 150 ° C and fry the chicken thighs for another 10 minutes until they are cooked.
5. The spicy chicken leg with barbecue marinade with corn salad and baguette serve.

Tip:

Preparation time: 5 minutes + 20 minutes for marinating + 20 minutes in the Philips Air fryer hot air fryer

Nutritional information :

- 610 kJ / 145 kcal
- 9 g protein
- 11 g total fat content
- 3 g of saturated fatty acids
- 2 g of carbohydrates
- 0 g fiber

Meatballs

Cooking time: 15 to 30 min

Ingredients:

Servings: 4

- 750 g Ground meat (mixed)
- 1 piece of bread (from the previous day)
- 2 pieces of onions (finely chopped)
- 1 tbsp parsley (finely chopped)
- 1 tbsp olive oil
- Salt
- 3 tbsp breadcrumbs
- Pepper

Preparation:

1. For the meatballs, soak the Semmelin water and squeeze out. Knead minced, crushed rolls, chopped onions, parsley and olive oil to a smooth mass season with salt and pepper.
2. Make small balls, roll them in the bread crumbs. Put the meatballs into vacuum-sealable bags 200 minutes at 200 ° C (without adding fat).
3. Serve the meatballs while still hot.

Tip:

The meatballs served with a dipping sauce of your choice.

Nutritional information :

- Calories 241
- % Daily Value
- Total Fat 15 G 23%
- Saturated Fat 6 G 30%
- Trans Fat 0.8 G
- Cholesterol 66 Mg 22%
- Sodium 73 Mg 3%
- Potassium 241 Mg 6%
- Total Carbohydrate 0 G 0%
- Dietary Fiber 0 G 0%
- Sugar 0 G

- Protein 24 G   48%

Spicy Meatballs with Fiery Dip

Cooking time: 15 to 30 min

Ingredients:

- Portions: 5
- 100 g fried sausages (fresh)
- 100 g of beef (beefsteak)
- 70 g breadcrumbs
- 1 piece of onion (small)
- 2 toes of garlic
- 1 piece egg
- 2 tablespoons parsley (chopped)
- 2 tbsp oil
- salt
- pepper
- Tabasco For the fiery dip:
- 2 pieces of onions
- 1 piece of peppers (red)
- 10 tablespoons tomato ketchup

- 5 pieces Gewürzgurkerl (vegetative fig leaf)
- 1 Tl mustard
- 1 pinch of sugar
- 1 pinch of cayenne pepper
- Tabasco

Preparation:

1. Skin the sausages and place in a bowl. Add beef, breadcrumbs and egg. Peel onions and cut them into fine pieces. Peel garlic and squeeze through the garlic press. Wash parsley, drain well and finely chop.
2. Add to the bowl and mix well all ingredients. Season well with salt, pepper and Tabasco. Make small balls (about 20 pieces) with wet hands. Vacuum-sealable bags with regular turning until they are evenly brown. Poke on toothpicks, place on a plate and serve with the fiery dip.
3. For the fiery dip, cut onions, cucumbers and pepper in a lightning cutter. Add the remaining ingredients and stir well. Season with sugar, cayenne pepper and Tabasco.

Nutritional information :

- Calories 197
- % Daily Value
- Total Fat 9 g   13%
- Saturated fat 1.4 g 7%
- Polyunsaturated fat 4.7 g
- Monounsaturated fat 2.2 g
- Cholesterol 0 mg 0%
- Total Carbohydrate 8 g 2%
- Dietary fiber 4.6 g 18%
- Sugar 1.3 g
- Protein 21 g   42%

Duck thighs

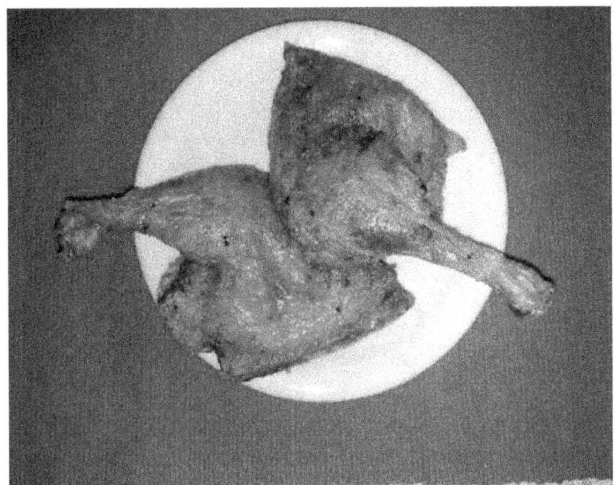

Cooking time: 30 to 60 min

Ingredients:

Servings: 2

- 2 pcs. Duck legs
- 1 tsp salt
- 1 tsp spice mixture (for ducks and geese)
- 1 tsp olive oil

Preparation:

1. For the duck legs of the vacuum-sealable bags and pat dry. Mix the oil with the salt and the spice mixture and rub the duck legs around with it.
2. Place the spiced duck legs on the rack of the vaccum and cook at 200 ° C in 40 minutes. After 20 minutes, turn the legs once.

Colorful Chicken Pans

Ingredients:

- 500 g   chopped chicken
- 2 pck. Vegetables (creamy vegetables), TK
- 125 ml Crème fine for cooking
- 4 tbsp soy sauce

Preparation:

Cooking time: about 10 minutes /. : Hot time approx. 15 minutes rest time: about 2 hours

1. Marinate the chicken with the soy sauce and let stand for 1 - 2 hours.
2. Add the meat with the soy into sauce vacuum-sealable bags. cook for 30 minutes while stirring between.
3. In a separate vacuum-sealable bags, add the creamy vegetables and creamy-fines and cook for another 10 minutes. Stir in between, so that the sauce is well distributed and nothing gets dry.
4. Finally, season to taste and serve.

Quick Crunchy Duck on Grilled Vegetables

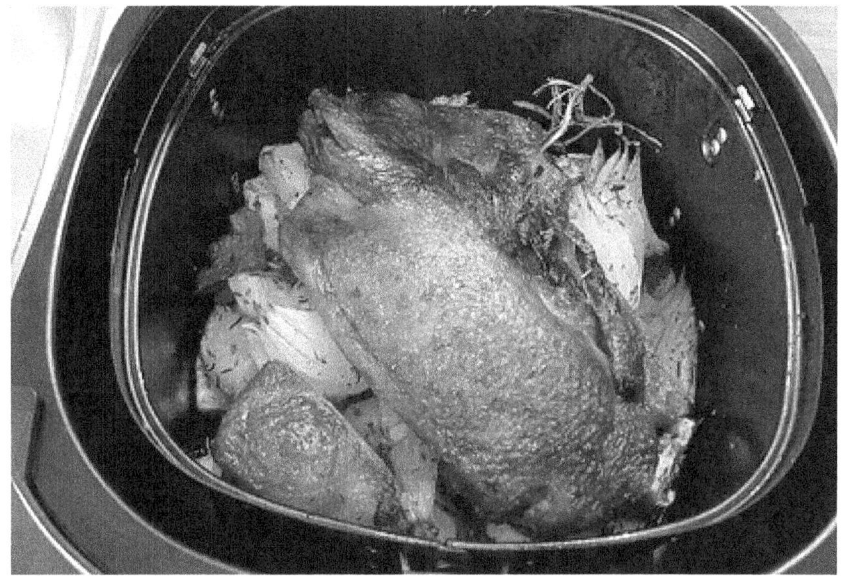

Ingredients:

- 300 g Duck (s), boneless, seasoned and pre-cooked
- 3 m. Large Potato (n)
- 1 Pepper (s), red
- 1 m. –Large zucchini
- 1 Onion (n)
- 2 toe / n garlic
- 2 tbsp olive oil
- 1 teaspoon Thyme, dried
- 1 / 2 tsp   Oregano, dried
- 1 stalk Rosemary, fresh
- 1 teaspoon Salt, coarse
- Pepper, freshly ground

Preparation:

1. Working time: approx. 5 min. / Cooking / baking time: approx. 50 min.

2. Place in separate vacuum-sealable bags and pour into the bags.
3. Prepare the sous vide immersion circulator for use according to the instructions. Preheat water to 126°F (52°C).
4. Place the bags to the circulating water and cook for 30 minutes for medium doneness.
5. Carefully take out the bags from the circulating water. Remove menu from the bags and pat dry

Nutritional Information:

- Calories 337
- % Daily Value
- Total Fat 28 g 43%
- Total Carbohydrate 0 g 0%
- Dietary fiber 0 g 0%
- Sugar 0 g
- Protein 19 g   38%

Mediterranean meatball

Ingredients:

- 80 g   Bread or rolls, stale
- 100 ml whole milk
- 1 pinch nutmeg
- Shallot (s), finely diced
- 2 tbsp olive oil
- 300 g Minced meat, mixed
- (S) Egg
- 1 tbsp Dijon mustard
- 1 tsp, heaped Paprika (Pimento de la Vera, smoked paprika powder)
- 30 g thyme
- 50 g Parmesan, grated
- 50 g Tomato (s), dried, finely chopped
- 1 Lemon (s), of which the abrasion
- 1 pinch sea-salt
- 1 pinch pepper from the grinder

Preparation:

1. Working time: approx. 15 min. / Cooking / baking time: approx. 10 min.
2. Place in separate vacuum-sealable bags and pour into the bags.
3. Prepare the sous vide immersion circulator for use according to the instructions. Preheat water to 126°F (52°C).
4. Put the bags in the circulating water and cook for 30 minutes for medium doneness.
5. Carefully remove bags from the water. Remove the menu from the bags and put them to dry.

Nutritional Information:

Amount Per 100 grams

- Calories 197

- % Daily Value
- Total Fat 9 g   13%
- Total Carbohydrate 8 g 2%
- Dietary fiber 4.6 g 18%
- Sugar 1.3 g
- Protein 21 g 42%

Steak Entrecote

Ingredients:

- 4 Steaks (s)
- tbsp oil
- Salt And Pepper

Preparation:

Working time: approx. 15 min. / Cooking / baking time: approx. 10 min.

1. Place in separate vacuum-sealable bags and pour into the bags.

2. Prepare the sous vide immersion circulator for use according to the instructions. Preheat water to 126°F (52°C).
3. Put the bags in the circulating water and cook for 30 minutes for medium doneness.
4. Carefully remove bags from the water. Remove the menu from the bags and put them to dry.

Carrots, Easy and Healthy Garnish

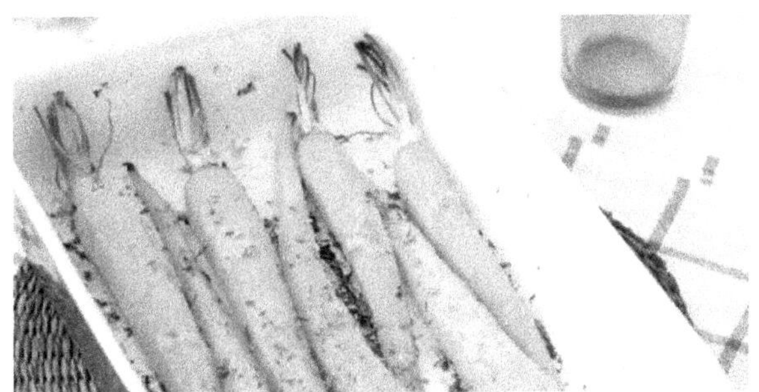

Preparation: 5 min   Cooking: 45 min   Difficulty: 1/5   Rations: 2-4

Ingredients:

- Tender Carrots, 7 or 8
- Extra virgin olive oil, ½ tablespoon
- Butter, 1 tbsp
- Salt
- Pepper
- Lemon juice, 2 tablespoons
- Thyme, 1 teaspoon

Preparation:

Working time: approx. 15 min. / Cooking / baking time: approx. 10 min.

1. Place in separate vacuum-sealable bags and pour into the bags.

2. Prepare the sous vide immersion circulator for use according to the instructions. Preheat water to 126°F (52°C).
3. Put the bags in the circulating water and cook for 30 minutes for medium doneness.
4. Carefully remove bags from the water. Remove the menu from the bags and put them to dry.
5. Serve cooked carrots with dried thyme on top.

Nutritional Information:

- 9% Total Fat 5.8g.
- 4% Saturated Fat 0.8g.
- 0% Cholesterol 0mg.
- 24% Sodium 574mg.
- 14% Potassium 480mg.
- 5% Total Carbohydrates 14g.
- 17% Dietary Fiber 4.2g.
- Sugars 7g.

Peppers Stuffed With Potato Omelet

Peppers stuffed with potato omelet are a quick dish to prepare, healthy and delicious. The flavor of the pepper combined with the potato omelet makes it one of the favorite recipes for many.

Stuffed tortilla peppers can be cooked without fat thanks to the Air fryer. The filling of the peppers can be changed to the taste of the diner. You can practically fill it with almost everything.

Ingredients:

For 4 servings

- 2 large peppers
- 2 medium potatoes
- 1 egg
- olive oil to taste
- salt to taste

Preparation: of tortilla-filled peppers

Preparation: time 30 min

1. Place in separate vacuum-sealable bags and pour into the bags.
2. Prepare the sous vide immersion circulator for use according to the instructions. Preheat water to 126°F (52°C).
3. Put the bags into the circulating water and cook for 30 minutes for medium doneness.
4. Carefully take out the bags from the circulating water. Remove the menu from the bags and put them to dry.
5. This recipe is quite flexible; it can be made with green, red or yellow peppers. You can add more with red pepper since the taste is sweeter. For a more intense flavor, green peppers are recommended. The filling on this occasion is with potato omelet but it can also be made with mushrooms or vegetables. Enjoy your meal!

Nutritional Information:

- Fat: 20.11 g
- Saturated fatty acids: 11 g
- Protein / protein: 14.49 g
- Roughage: 9.02 g
- Added sugar: 0 g
- Calories: 474

Rosti (Swiss potatoes)

Rations for four people:

Preparation: time: 10 m, cooking time 15m

Ingredients:

- 250 g peeled white potatoes
- 1 tablespoon finely chopped chives
- Freshly ground black pepper
- 1 tablespoon of olive oil
- 2 tablespoons of sour cream

Preparation:

1. Place in separate vacuum-sealable bags and pour into the bags.
2. Prepare sous vide immersion circulator for use according to the manufacturer's directions. Preheat water to 126°F (52°C).
3. Put the bags in the circulating water then cook it for 30 minutes for medium doneness.
4. Remove the bags from the circulating water. Remove the menu from the bags and put them to dry. Cut the rosti into 4 quarters and place each quarter on a plate. Garnish with a spoonful of sour cream. Spread the remaining of the scallions over the sour cream and add a touch of ground pepper.

Nutritional Information:

- Carbs: 25.2g
- Fat: 11.7g
- Fatty sat: 5.9g
- Protein: 2.5g
- Fibers: 1.9g
- Sugar: 2.2g
- Pro Points: 6
- Smart Points: 8

Ratatouille

Rations 4 people, Preparation: time: 8 m, cooking time 15 m

Ingredients:

- 200 g of zucchini and eggplant
- 1 yellow bell pepper
- 2 tomatoes
- 1 peeled onion
- 1 clove of crushed garlic
- 2 teaspoons dried Provencal herbs
- Freshly ground black pepper
- 1 tablespoon of olive oil

Instructions:

1. Place in separate vacuum-sealable bags and pour into the bags.
2. Prepare the sous vide immersion circulator for use according to the instructions. Preheat water to 126°F (52°C).
3. Place the bags into the circulating water and cook for 30 minutes for medium doneness.

4. Carefully take out the bags from the circulating water. Remove the menu from the bags and put them to dry. Serve it.

Nutritional Information:

- Calories: 76 kcal
- Proteins: 2 g
- Carbohydrates: 8 g

Mediterranean Recipes

Ingredients:

- Garlic
- Tomatoes
- Onion
- Vegetables
- Potatoes
- Yoghurt
- Water
- Lemon juice
- Salt and pepper
- Rosemary sprigs

Preparation:

1. Wash the small potatoes and then pre-cook in boiling salted water for 8 minutes. Drain the potatoes and cut in half. Clean the vegetables and cut into pieces. Remove the onion and diced. Peel off the garlic clove and chop finely. Wash the date tomatoes, but leave them alone.
2. Now put the potatoes, the chopped vegetables, tomatoes, onions and garlic in a baking dish. Season the salt and pepper, add the rosemary sprigs and mix again. Give olive oil over it.
3. Place in separate vacuum-sealable bags and pour into the bags.
4. Prepare sous vide immersion circulator for use according to the manufacturer's directions. Preheat at water to 126°F (52°C).
5. Put the bags in the circulating water then cook it for 30 minutes for medium doneness.
6. Remove the bags from circulating water. Remove the menu from the bags and put them to dry. Serve it.
7. Meanwhile mix together the yoghurt, the light mayonnaise and the lemon juice and season with salt and pepper.
8. The yoghurt dressing for Mediterranean grilled vegetables is enough. The grilled vegetables with the potatoes taste both warm and cold. Therefore, it is also ideal for party buffets or takeaway!

Nutritional Information:

- Kcal 439
- kJ 1842
- protein 16 g
- fat 7 g
- carbohydrates 76 g

Pumpkin seed Cheesecake

A hearty pumpkin seed cheesecake succeeds and tastes great and small. The recipe is of course prepared with curd cheese.

Ingredients for 8 servings:

- 100 G shortbread
- 30 G grated pumpkin seeds
- 80 G Flour
- 120 G Butter (room temperature)
- 30 ml pumpkin seed oil PGI
- 60 G icing sugar
- 3 stk eggs
- Ingredients for the abundance
- 500 G plugs
- 150 G sour cream
- 150 ml whipped cream
- 30 ml pumpkin seed oil PGI
- 180 G icing sugar
- 2 EL Flour
- 0.5 stk vanilla bean
- Ingredients for the garnish
- 6 stk strawberries
- 1 prize sugar
- 1 shot lemon juice
- 1 prize pumpkin seed brittle

- 1 shot Woodruff or lemon balm

Preparation:

1. Put the biscuits inside a freezer bag and pound with a mallet. Pumpkin seeds, flour, pumpkin seed oil PGI, butter, icing sugar and knead.
2. Butter a cake, fill with 3/4 of the mass and spread evenly with a spoon (press down a bit). Press a thin edge on the spring forming wall with the remaining dough. Put the cake tin in the fridge for about 2 hours.
3. Place in separate vacuum-sealable bags and pour into the bags.
4. Place in separate vacuum-sealable bags and pour into the bags.
5. Prepare sous vide immersion circulator for use according to the manufacturer's directions. Preheat at water to 126°F (52°C).
6. Put the bags in the circulating water then cook it for 30 minutes for medium doneness.
7. Remove the bags from circulating water. Remove the menu from the bags and put them to dry. Serve it.
8. Cut strawberries into small pieces, marinate with sugar and lemon juice. Distribute evenly on the cheese cake, sprinkle with pumpkin seed and icing sugar with Styrian power.

Tips on the recipe:

- Garnish as desired with woodruff or lemon balm.
- Nutritional Information:
- Kcal 439
- kJ 1842
- protein 16 g
- fat 7 g
- carbohydrates 76 g

Lentil stew

Ingredients:

Servings: 2

- 500 g of potatoes
- 100 g lentils (dried)
- 1 piece of onion
- 1 piece of carrot
- 70 g celeriac
- 1 tbsp rapeseed oil
- Vegetable stock cube
- Lobeerblatt
- 100 ml of lean yoghurt
- Parsley (chopped)

Preparation:

1. For the lentil stew, soak the lenses overnight in 1/2 l of water.
2. Drain lean yogurt in the coffee filter.

3. Cut onions into rings. Place the mixture into a bags in the circulating water and then cook it for 30 minutes for medium doneness.
4. Remove the bags from the circulating water. Remove the menu from the bags and put them to dry. Add lentils with soaking water, add vegetable soup and bay leaf, cook for about 20 minutes.
5. Dice carrots into slices and celery; add cooking time after 10 minutes.
6. Arrange stew in deep plates with potatoes, serve with a layer of skinny yoghurt and sprinkle with chopped parsley.
7. Instead of potatoes, bread dumplings also go well with lentil stew.
8. If you need to go fast, you can also use lentils (500 g) instead of dried lentils.

Nutritional Information:

- Calories 241
- 1% Saturated Fat 0.2g grams
- Trans Fat 0g grams
- 0%Cholesterol 0mg milligrams
- 15%Total Carbohydrates 45g grams
- 64% Dietary Fiber 16g grams
- Protein 16g grams
- 57% Vitamin A
- 37% Vitamin C
- 10% Calcium
- 38% Iron

Watermelons Fruit Sushi

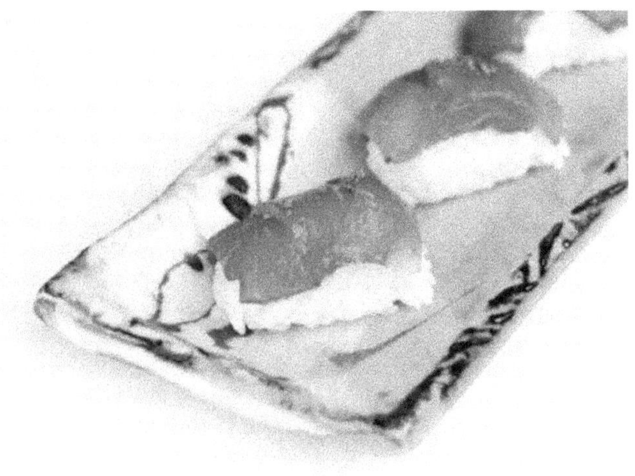

Cooking time: 30 to 60 min

Ingredients:

Servings: 10

- 1 piece of watermelon (should be enough for 20 slices of 5 x 2.5 cm)
- 1 piece of lemon (juice of it)
- 10 g of sugar
- Basil leaves (fresh or dried)
- 1/2 serving of lemon rice

Preparation:

1. For the watermelon Fruit sushi, cut the watermelon into thin slices and marinate for five to ten minutes in the mixture of lemon juice and sugar.
2. Place the melon slices on a baking sheet lined with baking paper and Place them in the vacuum-sealable bags and pour into the bags.

3. Place in separate vacuum-sealable bags and pour into the bags.
4. Prepare sous vide immersion circulator for use according to the manufacturer's directions. Preheat at water to 126°F (52°C).
5. Put the bags in the circulating water then cook it for 30 minutes for medium doneness.
6. Remove the bags from circulating water. Remove the menu from the bags and put them to dry.
7. Of lemon rice form and put on it the melon slices with the grilled side down. Sprinkle with a pinch of chopped basil and serve the watermelon Fruit sushi.

Tip:

After a few minutes under the grill, the watermelon gets a very special color and texture, which reminds a bit of tuna. If you have guests, let them try and guess what's on the fruit sushi before you reveal the secret of the watermelon Fruit sushi.

Blueberry pancakes

Ingredients:

Servings: 2

- 3 egg whites
- 1 tbsp sugar
- 125 ml of milk
- 65 g of flour
- 3 egg yolks
- 80 g blueberries
- 40 g almond slivers
- lemon juice
- 1 shot of rum (or Rumaroma)
- 1 tbsp vanilla sugar
- 1 pinch of salt
- 1 tsp butter
- Icing sugar (for dusting)

Preparation:

1. For the blueberry pancake in a bowl, beat the egg whites with sugar until they are solid.
2. In another bowl, add milk, flour, egg yolks, blueberries, almonds, lemon juice, rum, vanilla sugar and a pinch of salt until smooth.
3. Gently lift the egg whites under the dough. Add 1 tsp butter to the dish, pour the dough into the vacum at 180 ° C for 10-13 minutes.
4. Dust the dust with icing sugar and allow caramelizing for another 5 minutes.
5. Then remove the insert and pluck the blueberry pancake with 2 wooden spoons.
6. To match cranberries and applesauce.

You can do this putty all year round. Simply replace the blueberries with a fruit that is currently in season.

Cooked Oven Vegetables

Ingredients:

Servings: 2

- 1 pc paprika (red)
- 1 pc paprika (yellow)
- 1 piece of zucchini
- 1 piece of onion (red)
- Olive oil (something)
- 1 teaspoon sea salt
- pepper
- 2 tbsp sugar (possibly icing sugar)
- 1/2 bunch of thyme (leaves removed and chopped)

Preparation:

1. For the cooked oven vegetables, wash the vegetables and dry with kitchen paper. Cut into cubes and marinate in a bowl with oil, sea salt and the sugar.
2. Add the thyme to the vegetables and mix in a bowl.
3. Place the marinated vegetables on the grid and cook in the vaccum at 180 ° C for 15-18 minutes.
4. The cooked roasted vegetables served with fresh herbs sprinkled.

As an additional ingredient, you can also add ricotta or cottage cheese to the cooked oven vegetables so you have a complete meal.

Pearl barley sweet potato salad with raisins

Cooking time: 30 to 60 min

Ingredients:

Portions: 1

- 50 g pearl barley
- 1 sweet potato
- 2 tablespoons raisins
- 10 g of hemp seeds (peeled)

- 1 Apple of paradise
- 5 leaves of parsley
- 4 tablespoons apple aronia juice
- 1-2 tbsp of hempseed oil
- 1 tablespoon of apple cider vinegar
- 10 leaves of mint
- salt

Preparation:

1. For the pearl barley sweet potato salad with raisins, first prick the sweet potato with a fork several times and cook in the vaccum at 160 ° C for about 30 minutes, when it is soft, remove from the air fryer, allow to cool and crush the meat with a fork ,
2. Coarsely chop the parsley, quarter the parade, cut out the core and cut the pulp into cubes.
3. Boil the pearl barley inside plenty of salted water until soft, drain and chill, add the sweet potato, raisins, hemp seeds, parsley and lemon dice and season to taste with apple aronia juice, hemp seed oil, apple cider vinegar and salt. The pearl barley sweet potato salad with raisins garnish with fresh mint.

Tip:

Super plus: The fiber in the pearl barley sweet potato salad with raisins lasts longer.

Effect: High fiber meals increase the volume of the food pulp. The duration of digestion is prolonged, which also leads to a longer lasting feeling of satiety: for a weight reduction of great importance.

Nutritional Information:

- Calories: 596kcal

- Carbohydrates: 67.5g
- Protein: 10.5g
- Fat: 34.5g
- Saturated Fat: 4.3g
- Cholesterol: 0mg
- Fiber: 14.6g

Snow dumpling with vanilla milk and fruit salad

Cooking time: 15 to 30 min

Ingredients:

Servings: 4

- 3 eggs
- 90 g of fine crystalline sugar
- 500 ml of milk
- 60 g icing sugar
- 1 pod of vanilla (scratched out)
- 1 pinch of salt
- Fruits (optional, season)
- 1-2 tbsp honey
- 1-2 tablespoons of lemon juice

Preparation:

1. Separate eggs for the snow dumplings from the hot fryer. For the dumplings, beat egg whites with salt until they are light, gradually add the granulated sugar until it has dissolved (test it with the finger) and a very stiff, shiny egg whites has been produced.
2. Add the milk with icing sugar and scraped-out vanilla seeds to the pan, stir until smooth and heat at 180 ° C for about 5 minutes in Hot Fryer.
3. Using a pair of moistened spoons, make a dumpling out of the egg whites and place in the heated milk. Leave to cook in the vaccum for about 3-4 minutes at about 90 ° C (do not boil!). Lift dumplings out of the vanilla milk. Finally, stir the yolks quickly into the non-boiling, hot milk.
4. Wash fruits, cut into bite-sized pieces and season with honey and lemon juice.
5. Arrange fruit salad in deep plates, put snowball from the hot air fryer and drizzle with a little vanilla milk.
6. Serve with seasonal fruit and flavor possibly sprinkle with almonds or pistachios.

Delicious oven vegetables

No matter what time of year, colorful oven vegetables are always in season with us. Sure, not every season you always get the same fresh ingredients, but that does not matter.

Because the nice thing about tasty oven vegetables is that you can vary the ingredients according to your mood.

For this recipe, here are selected the following ingredients.

Ingredients:

- zucchini
- mushrooms
- paprika
- aubergine Vegetable
- carrots
- olive oil
- salt
- pepper
- Paprika powder (sweet)
- Parsley for garnish

Preparation:

1. First, the vegetables are cleaned and crushed. Clean the zucchini and slice. Clean mushrooms and quarter them. Wash the peppers and separate into strips. Clean eggplant and cut into cubes. Peel carrots and slice.
2. All the vegetables are now added directly to the the vacuum-sealable bags and pour into the bags.
3. Prepare sous vide immersion circulator for use according to the manufacturer's directions. Preheat at water to 126°F (52°C).
4. Put the bags in the circulating water then cook it for 30 minutes for medium doneness.
5. Remove the bags from circulating water. Remove the menu from the bags and put them to dry.

6. Now the marinade is being prepared. For this we mix about 5 tablespoons of good olive oil with salt, pepper and the paprika powder. This marinade is now added directly to the vegetables and stirred once.

7. Now it's ready to go. We set a temperature of 180 degrees on our hot air fryer and set the timer to 30 minutes. Of course, depending on the device and the quantity, the cooking time can also increase slightly. Now we press Start.

8. With all the recipes for hot air fryers, it is not always that easy, since everyone has a different device.

9. Accordingly, you have to play around with temperature and time until you find the right setting for your own device. But continue in the text. Halfway through, we stir vigorously and let the vegetables cook for the rest of the time.

10. Once the time has elapsed, you will quickly check whether everything is already there. If that is the case, it can already be served

Simple fruit salad

Cooking time: 15 to 30 min

Ingredients:

- Portions: 1
- 1 piece of pear
- 1 piece of apple
- 1 piece of banana
- Sesame
- Cinnamon

Preparation:

1. For the fruit salad, first cut all fruits into small pieces and mix in a bowl. Sprinkle cinnamon and sesame on top and place in the sous vide immersion circulator for use according to the manufacturer's instructions for few minutes to steam, then delicious snack is ready in between.

Tip:

- With honey, the fruit salad tastes great too!

Nutritional Information:

- Calories 97
- 1%Total Fat 0.5g grams
- 0% Saturated Fat 0.1g grams
- Trans Fat 0g grams
- Polyunsaturated Fat 0.2g grams
- Monounsaturated Fat 0.1g grams
- 0%Cholesterol 0mg milligrams
- 0%Sodium 2.6mg milligrams
- 10%Potassium 364mg milligrams
- 8%Total Carbohydrates 24g grams
- 13% Dietary Fiber 3.3g grams
- Sugars 16g grams
- Protein 1.4g grams
- 1.9% Vitamin A
- 120% Vitamin C

- 2% Calcium
- 2.9% Iron

Salad of baby carrots

Cooking time: 30 to 60 min

Ingredients:

For the salad:

- 160 g baby carrots
- 250 ml vegetable stock
- 1 tsp coffee beans
- 1 tsp ginger (freshly grated)
- 1 orange
- Corn salad (or Frisée)
- Chervil (fresh)
- Basil (fresh)
- Lemon verbena (fresh)

For the marinade:

- 2 tbsp Chardonnay vinegar (white wine vinegar, as an alternative juice from a lime)
- 6 tbsp olive oil (organic)
- 2 Msp. Tonka bean (alternatively a vanilla pod)
- sea-salt
- honey

- For the espresso tour:
- 100 g of butter
- 50 g of sugar
- 3 eggs
- 2 egg yolks
- 1-2 oranges
- lemon juice
- Lemon peel

Preparation:

2. For the salad of baby carrots, first wash carrots and sauté in a container with a little oil.
3. Add coffee beans and stir fry.
4. Then add vegetable stock and freshly grated ginger and cook until firm.
5. Wash the salad and mix with lemon verbena, fresh chervil and basil. Fillet the orange and add the orange fillets.
6. For the marinade stir together chardonnay vinegar, organic olive oil, tonka beans, a little sea salt and honey. Then individually season the salad with the marinade and place into the vaccum for few seconds.
7. For the espresso toast, squeeze oranges and mix with the double espresso to 300 ml of juice.
8. Then melt the butter in the pot and mix with lemon juice, lemon peel and sugar. Whisk the eggs, whisk well and pour through a fine sieve into the pot. Stir the mixture over medium heat with an sous vide vaccum until it thickens to a cream and then cold. It is important not to let the mass boil and stir firmly so that it does not burn.
9. Arrange the cooked carrots with the salad and serve salad of baby carrots.

Nutritional Information:

- Calories 41

- Protein 0.9 g
- Carbs   9.6 g
- Fat   0.2 g

Potato Gratin

Cooking time: 15 to 30 min

Ingredients:

Servings: 4

- 400 g potatoes (slightly floury, peeled)
- 50 ml of milk
- 50 ml whipping cream
- Pepper (freshly ground)
- Nutmeg
- 40 g Gruyere cheese (or middle-aged cheese, grated)

Preparation:

1. For the potato gratin, cut the potatoes into thin slices.

2. Mix the milk in a bowl with whipped cream and season with salt, pepper and nutmeg. Turn the sliced potatoes in the milk mixture.
3. Put the slices of potatoes in a slightly oiled quiche (15 cm diameter) and pour the rest of the topping from the bowl over the potatoes. Distribute the cheese evenly over the potatoes.
4. Place the quiche dish in the cooking basket and push the basket into the sous vides vaccum. Set the timer to 15-18 minutes and bake the potato gratin at 200°C, until it is beautifully browned and cooked.

Preparation: time: 10 minutes + 15 minutes

Nutritional Information:

- Calories 323
- 29% Total Fat 18.6g
- 58% Saturated Fat 11.6g
- 19% Cholesterol 56mg
- 46% Sodium 1061mg
- 9% Total Carbohydrate 27.6g
- 16% Dietary Fiber 4.4g
- Protein 12.4g
- 13% Vitamin A 647 IU
- 40% Vitamin C 24mg
- 29% Calcium 292mg
- 9% Iron 1.6mg

Vegetable Burgers

Cooking time: 30 to 60 min

Ingredients:

- 250g vegetables (carrots, zucchini, leeks, peas, corn, carob,)
- 70 g of oatmeal (roughly chopped)
- 20 g of butter
- 125 ml of milk
- 1-piece egg
- 100 g crumbs (of debarked white bread)
- salt
- pepper
- marjoram
- 1 tbsp parsley (freshly chopped)
- Crumbs (to roll)
- Oil (or clarified butter for frying)

Preparation:

1. Depending on the consistency, grate the vegetables roughly or cut them into small pieces and possibly boil them up. Sweat the oats in butter, pour milk on them and

let them boil down. Let cool down. Then mix with vegetables and the egg and tie with the crumbs. Season with spicy salt, pepper, marjoram and parsley.

2. From the mass patties (small patties) form, dip one side in breadcrumbs and sous vide vaccum.
3. Suggested side: Tomato or warm or cold herb sauce, the patties can also be served as a side dish to vegetable dishes with sauce.

Nutritional Information:

- Calories 177
- Total Fat 6 g 9%
- Saturated fat 1.4 g 7%
- Polyunsaturated fat 2 g
- Monounsaturated fat 1.8 g
- Cholesterol 5 mg
- Sodium 569 mg
- Potassium 333 mg
- Total Carbohydrate 14 g
- Dietary fiber 4.9 g
- Sugar 1.1 g
- Protein 16 g
- Vitamin A 0%
- Vitamin C 7%
- Calcium 13%
- Iron 13%
- Vitamin D 0%
- Vitamin B-6 15%

Pumpkin Puffs with Yoghurt Dip

Cooking time: 15 to 30 min

Ingredients:

Servings: 4

- 1 pumpkin (best Hokkaido)
- 3 tbsp sunflower oil
- some curry powder
- some French fry salt for the yoghurt dip:
- 250 g yoghurt
- 1/2 clove garlic (squeezed)
- Salt
- Pepper (from the mill)

Preparation:

1. First wash the squash for the pumpkin puffs, cut in the middle and remove the pits (Hokkaido does not have to be peeled, other pumpkin varieties already). Cut into thin slices. Brush with the oil and sprinkle half each with curry powder or French spiced salt.

2. Cook in sous vide vaccum at 200 ° C for about 15 minutes until crisp.
3. In the meantime, mix for the dip all ingredients.
4. The pumpkin fries with yoghurt dip serve.
5. The pumpkin fries with yoghurt dip served as a snack or side dish.

Nutritional Information:

- Calories 130
- 4% Total Fat 2.5g
- 8% Saturated Fat 1.5g
- Trans Fat 0g
- 5% Cholesterol 15mg
- 3% Sodium 60mg
- 5% Total Carbohydrate 16g
- 0% Dietary Fiber 0g
- Sugars 12g
- Protein 12g
- 8% Vitamin A 400 IU
- 0% Vitamin C 0mg
- 15% Calcium 150mg
- 0% Iron 0mg
- 6% Potassium 220mg

Herbal Foam Soup with Crispy Egg

An herbal foam soup with a crunchy egg has to be tried once, the recipe to cook for a great appetizer.

Ingredients for 8 servings

- 2 EL butter
- 1 stk Onion (finely diced)
- 125 ml White wine
- 2 stk Potatoes (peeled and diced)
- 1.5 l vegetable stock
- 250 ml whipped cream
- 250 G wild garlic
- 1 prize salt and pepper
- Ingredients for the crispy egg
- 8 stk eggs
- 1 prize salt
- 80G pumpkin seeds (chopped)
- 2 stk Eggs (bubbled)
- 80 g bread crumbs
- 80 g flour

Preparation:

1. In a saucepan, sauté the onion until glassy and add the diced potatoes and sweat briefly. Deglaze with white wine, pour on a vegetable stock and simmer. Season with salt, pepper and Mukat. Cook until the potatoes are soft. Add the upper garlic and wild garlic, bring to a boil with sous vide vaccum, puree and season to taste.
2. Lay out a suitable shape with cling film and beat in the egg. Knot foil, no more air in the foil. Put the egg in boiling water for about 5-6 minutes. Then immediately quench with cold water and remove the foil. Salt the eggs and bread them in flour, egg and bread crumbs pumpkin seed and bake in air fryer until golden brown.
3. Serving: Place the halved egg in the center of the soup plate. Froth the soup with the hand blender and pour it next to the egg. Garnish with chopped wild garlic and serve.
4. Tips on the recipe
5. Alternatively to wild garlic, parsley, chives or wild herbs can be used.

- Nutritional Information:
- Energy 307 kcal 15.4%
- Fat/Lipids 13 g 19.2%
- Saturated Fats 1.5 g 7.5%
- Carbohydrates 35 g 13.0%
- Sugars 9.1 g 10.1%
- Fiber 14 g 55.9%
- Protein (albumin) 15 g 29.9%
- Cooking Salt 559 mg 23.3%

Pumpkin Seed Oil Parfait with Strawberry

A great pumpkin seed parfait with strawberry not only looks great, it also tastes great. This recipe belongs in every recipe collection.

Ingredients for 4 servings:

- 100 g strawberries (fresh or frozen, for pureeing)
- 125 g strawberries (fresh if possible)
- 1 EL sugar
- 1 stk egg
- 1 stk yolk
- 100 G sugar
- 40 ml pumpkin seed oil PGI
- 200 ml whipped cream
- 2 EL pumpkin seed brittle

Preparation:

1. Put 100g of fresh strawberries in a bowl, add sugar, puree well. Cut the remaining strawberries into cubes and stir into the strawberry sauce and refine with stripped mint or basil.
2. Beat the egg and yolk with the sugar until creamy until a firm mass is formed. Carefully stir in the Styrian pumpkin

seed oil PGI and the Styrian pumpkin seed brittle. Now fold in the beaten upper. Fill into appropriate muffins and refrigerate for a few hours or overnight in the freezer.

3. Dip the parfaits with the parfait in sous vide vaccum at a warm degree and arrange on the plates with the strawberry.
4. Tips on the recipe
5. If TK strawberries are used, let them thaw first.

Nutritional Information:

- Contains 760 Kcal
- 11g Protein
- 47g Carbohydrates
- 58g Fat

Summer stir-fry tray

Ingredients:

- Stir fry dish with pineapple
- 3 medium-sized potatoes
- 10 cm chorizo sausage
- 1/3 fresh pineapple
- 125 grams of champignons

- Fresh herbs, parsley and chives or others to taste.
- olive oil
- pepper and salt

Preparation:

1. Peel the potatoes and rinse them under the tap. Cut them into thin slices and then into cubes. Put some olive oil in a large frying pan and put in the potato pieces (or use vacuum-sealable bags). As you continue to cut, shake the ingredients in the pan every now and then. Cut the chorizo into slices and then the slices into quarters. Add. Cut the mushrooms into slices and add. Remove the pineapple from the peel and cut into small pieces. Add it too. Stir fry as long as necessary, until everything is cooked. Cut the herbs above the pan and stir fry briefly.

This is enough for 2 people and 1 child. Tasty with a green salad.

Mexican rice

Recipe for 2 people

Time: 25 min.

Ingredients:

- 150 gr of rice
- 200 gr minced meat (possibly more minced)
- 200 gr Mexican vegetables (eg kidney beans, corn and red onion)
- 1 can of corn (140 gr)
- 1 can of tomato paste (70 gr)
- 1 onion
- 1 pepper
- half tb cumin
- pinch of salt and pepper
- 1 tsp paprika powder
- 250 ml of water (possibly more if necessary)
- half bouillon cube (garden herbs)
- 1 red pepper

Preparation method:

1. Cut the pepper, onion and red pepper into pieces. Pour a dash of oil into a pan and fry the minced meat with a pinch of salt and pepper. Then add the pepper, onion and red pepper and fry for a few minutes. Then add the Mexican vegetables, the corn and the tomato paste. Mix together and place them in the vacuum-sealable bags and pour into the bags.
2. Prepare sous vide immersion circulator for use according to the manufacturer's directions. Preheat at water to 126°F (52°C).
3. Put the bags in the circulating water then cook it for 30 minutes for medium doneness.
4. Remove the bags from circulating water. Remove the menu from the bags and put them to dry.

Broad beans in a rice pan

Preparation:

- Olive oil
- 400 g mushroom stir-fry mix or 250 grams of mushrooms, a leek and a red onion.
- 3 tl dragon

- 275 g nut rice
- 700 ml vegetable stock
- 250 gram fresh broad beans or frozen beans
- 1 organic lemon
- 100 grams dairy spread light natural
- spring onions
- Salt and pepper

Preparation:

1. Choose a pan with a thick bottom and add some olive oil. Put the red onion, the leek and the mushrooms (the stir fry mix) in the pan and sprinkle the tarragon over them. Stir fry for about a minute on a high heat. Add the rice and the stock. The lid can be put on the pan and let the dish cook for 12 minutes. After 8 minutes you can add the broad beans and let them cook. We had fresh broad beans. I think they can go into the pan earlier, because we thought they had a lot of bite now.
2. Time to grate the lemon, clean the lemon and grate the peel, remove the pan from the heat, place them in the vacuum-sealable bags and pour into the bags.
3. Prepare sous vide immersion circulator for use according to the manufacturer's directions. Preheat at water to 126°F (52°C).
4. Put the bags in the circulating water then cook it for 30 minutes for medium doneness.
5. Remove the bags from circulating water. Remove the menu from the bags and put them to dry. and serve immediately.
6. Enjoy your meal!

Paste with delicious chicken

Ingredients (for ± 4 people) :

- 300 grams of chicken fillet
- 300 grams of mushrooms
- 1 onion
- two cloves of garlic (or more if you love it, or of course less if you do not want to use garlic)
- 200 grams of bacon
- 450 ml chicken broth
- 225 ml of cooking cream
- 400 grams of pasta (I used macaroni)
- 200-250 grams of grated parmesan cheese
- spring onions

Preparation:

1. Cut the chicken into cubes, the onion into pieces, the mushrooms into pieces. Slice the garlic.
2. Fry the onion and garlic, then add the chicken, mushrooms and the bacon.
3. Place the chicken and the sauce into the vacuum-sealable bags and pour into the bags.
4. Prepare sous vide immersion circulator for use according to the manufacturer's directions. Preheat at water to 126°F (52°C).
5. Put the bags in the circulating water then cook it for 30 minutes for medium doneness.
6. Remove the bags from circulating water. Remove the menu from the bags and put them to dry. Ready to serve!
7. This dish is also tasty with leek. Then cut it into (half) rings and add at the same time as the mushrooms.

Kale with sausage

Ingredients for 4 people:

- 2 onions
- olive oil

- 1 beef broth
- 600gr stew potatoes
- 300gr kale
- 400gr kidney beans
- 1 or 2 smoked sausages
- soy sauce
- pepper
- salt

Preparation time: 30 minutes

1. Peel the onions and cut into thin half-moons.
2. Heat a large frying or soup pan that will fit all ingredients in the future. Fry the onion in 2 tablespoons of olive oil until they are glassy and brown.
3. Pour 1 liter of water into the pan and add the potatoes together with the beef stock cube. Bring to the boil and let the potatoes boil for 15 minutes. Then add the kale, stir through the moisture and let it cook for 5 minutes. Check the doneness and the moisture content, if necessary add some water.
4. In the meantime, rinse the brown beans in a colander and slice the smoked sausage into slices.
5. Lower the heat and stir in the brown beans and smoked sausage. Season to taste with a tablespoon of soy sauce.
6. Let it simmer for minutes in the sous vade vaccum or 2 and test. If necessary, add extra flavor to pepper, soy sauce or salt.
7. Spoon the portions with a soup spoon into a deep plate, taste even better with a little of the stock.

Mexican dish with sweet potato

Ingredients (2 - 3 people):

- 200 grams of low-fat ground beef
- 200 grams of sweet potato in cubes
- 1 small can of corn
- 1 small can of black beans
- 1 onion
- 1 clove of garlic
- 5 halved cherry tomatoes
- 1 avocado
- 1 forest onion
- 125 grams of sour cream
- 1 teaspoon of cumin powder
- ½ tsp cayenne pepper
- ½ tablespoon of paprika
- salt

Preparation:

1. Chop the onion nicely and finely chop the garlic. Fry these in a frying pan until the good starts the smells.
2. Put the sweet potato in the garlic and onion in the pan and fry it almost 15 minutes.

3. Add the minced meat to the sweet potato mix and scoop the whole. Bake the minced meat.
4. Rinse the corn and black beans well under the cold tap and add them together with the halved cherry tomatoes to the rest of the ingredients.
5. Put the cumin powder, cayenne pepper and paprika into the pan and scoop the whole. Season with a pinch of salt, heat the whole for five more minutes on medium heat.
6. Meanwhile cut the spring onion in rings and the avocado into cubes. Divide this over the pan with warm ingredients.
7. Place them in the vacuum-sealable bags and pour into the bags.
8. Prepare sous vide immersion circulator for use according to the manufacturer's directions. Preheat at water to 126°F (52°C).
9. Put the bags in the circulating water then cook it for 30 minutes for medium doneness.
10. Remove the bags from circulating water. Remove the menu from the bags and put them to dry.
11. Scoop the sour cream here and there over the meal and serve immediately.

Minced meat with leek and yoghurt

Ingredients for 3-4 people:

- 2 leeks
- 2 kohlrabi
- 300g minced beef
- 1/2 vegetable broth (preferably without or little salt)
- 175gr beans (optional), rinsed
- 1/2 clove of garlic
- 150ml yoghurt
- 1el Chopped Parsley
- Pinch of Cayenne Pepper
- 2el Seeds and Kernels (Eg Roasted Sunflower Seeds)
- Oil
- Sea Salt
- Pepper

Preparation:

1. Cut the leeks into rings, peel the kohlrabi and cut into cubes. Heat up one tablespoon of oil inside a frying pan and dissolve the minced meat here and season to taste with salt and pepper. Remove the minced meat from the pan and stir-fry the leeks and kohlrabi for 2 minutes. Add the minced meat again and add 300ml of water. Crumble the

bouillon cube on top, bring to the boil and simmer for 5 minutes with the lid on the pan. Add the beans for 2 minutes and stir them gently.

2. While the pan is simmering, grate the garlic over the yogurt. Stir in this together with half of the parsley and season with salt and pepper.
3. After 5 minutes, add a pinch of cayenne pepper to the minced meat pot, then try and bring to taste.
4. Note: When using the vacuum-sealable, Place them in the vacuum-sealable bags and pour into the bags.
5. Prepare sous vide immersion circulator for use according to the manufacturer's directions. Preheat at water to 126°F (52°C).
6. Put the bags in the circulating water then cook it for 30 minutes for medium doneness.
7. Remove the bags from circulating water. Remove the menu from the bags and put them to dry.
8. Serve with a spoonful of yoghurt and sprinkle some seeds and parsley over it. It is already delicious, but you can also serve some brown rice or bread.

Quinoa with Mexican vegetables

Ingredients for 4 people:

- 170gr quinoa

- 1 onion
- 2 garlic cloves
- 300gr chicken breast or chicken
- thighs - 1 can (310gr) tricolore bean mix
- 400gr paprika, cabbage and leeks combined or 1 bag of Mexican stir-fried vegetables
- olive oil
- 1el Mexican herbs (for example the picadillo spices of Jonnie / Original Spices or you make them yourself with this recipe)

Preparation time: 20 minutes

1. If you use regular quinoa, you cook it for about 12 minutes according to the instructions on the packaging. The pre-cooked quinoa is even easier, because you only have to pour some boiled water and let it sink.
2. Chop the onion and garlic and cut the chicken into cubes. Rinse the bean mix in a colander and let it drain. The vegetables are cut roughly or you open the bag with cut vegetables.
3. Grab a vacuum-sealable bags heat it. Pour 2 tablespoons of olive oil and fry the onion and garlic together with a full tablespoon of Mexican herbs. Then the pieces of chicken are added and you bake them all around brown. The vegetables can now be added and you wok for a few more minutes until everything is done. Now pour the beans and quinoa through, warm for a little while and serve.

Spaghetti with meatballs

Ingredients:

- 800 g americain nature
- 1 egg
- 1 shallot, chopped
- 60 g breadcrumbs
- 1 tbsp lyophilized basil
- pepper & salt
- olive oil
- 300 ml tomato sauce
- 400 g spaghetti
- 20 leaves basil

Preparation:

1. Mix the mince with the egg, shallot, breadcrumbs and basil and season with a lot of salt and pepper.
2. Form balls of the minced meat, using about 2 tablespoons of meat per ball. Put some olive oil in vacuum-sealable bags the balls brown. That should not last longer than 5 minutes.
3. Remove the balls, fill the pot with water and a pinch of salt. Cook the pasta al dente.

4. Drain the spaghetti, put it back in the pan and add the tomato sauce and balls. Finish with the basil leaves and simmer for a short while on a low heat.

Spaghetti primavera with feta

Ingredients:

- 400 g of spaghetti
- 1 zucchini
- 10 green asparagus
- 200 g peas (frozen or fresh)
- Olive oil
- 1 bunch of chives
- 1 broccoli
- 1 slice or feta
- Pepper and salt

Preparation:

1. Slice the zucchini, peel the asparagus and cut them in two. Cut the broccoli into small florets and fry the vegetables for about 10 minutes in a pan with some olive oil. Add salt and pepper.

2. Boil the spaghetti al dente in the vacuum-sealable bags with a pinch of salt. Then drain, but keep a little of the cooking water.
3. Add the vegetable mixture, and then add the peas and chives, some olive oil and 2 tablespoons of cooking water.
4. Heat the whole while stirring. Then crumble the feta and sprinkle over the spaghetti.

Rigatoni with mushrooms and chicken

Ingredients:

- 300 g mushrooms
- 2 cloves of garlic
- 300 g rigatoni
- 1 bunch of chives
- Pepper & salt
- 600 g chicken fillet
- 1 red pepper
- 1 onion
- 200 ml cream
- 100 g grated parmesan

Preparation:

1. Cut the chicken into cubes of about 3 cm by 3 cm. Cook with vacuum-sealable bags until tender and golden brown together with the finely chopped garlic, onion and red pepper.
2. Cook the pasta al dente in the same pan in water with a pinch of salt. Make while the mushrooms clean and cut into slices.
3. Add the pasta to the paprika, garlic and onion. Then add the mushrooms and let it fry. Then add the cream, chopped chives and parmesan and simmer for a moment.

Spinach pesto

Ingredients:

- 150 g spinach
- 8 basil leaves
- 2 garlic cloves
- Olive oil
- 75 g pumpkin seeds
- salt & pepper
- 400 g tagliatelle
- 100 g parmesan

Preparation:

1. Place everything together in the blender and mix.
2. Add some extra olive oil if the pesto is too thick.
3. Boil the tagliatelle al dente in vacuum-sealable bags with a pinch of salt. Drain the pasta, add the pesto and also 1 tablespoon of cooking liquid. Let simmer for another 2 minutes on a low heat.
4. Sprinkle parmesan to your heart's content.

Penne with pumpkin, goat cheese and walnuts

Ingredients:

- 1 large butternut
- 4 tablespoons of walnut oil
- 1 clove of garlic
- 50 g of walnuts
- 2 tablespoons of flat parsley
- pepper & salt
- 400 g of penne
- 75 g of creamy goat's cheese

Preparation:

1. Peel the pumpkin, and cook in vacuum-sealable bags with a few tablespoons of oil for half an hour.

2. Cook the penne al dente, and crush while the walnuts and cut the parsley and garlic.
3. Put the pumpkin together with some oil, the walnuts, parsley, garlic and the goat cheese in the pan in which you cooked the pasta. Heat for 3 minutes and stir well until the pumpkin is crushed.
4. Season with pepper & salt.

Penne with tomatoes, peppers, olives and bacon

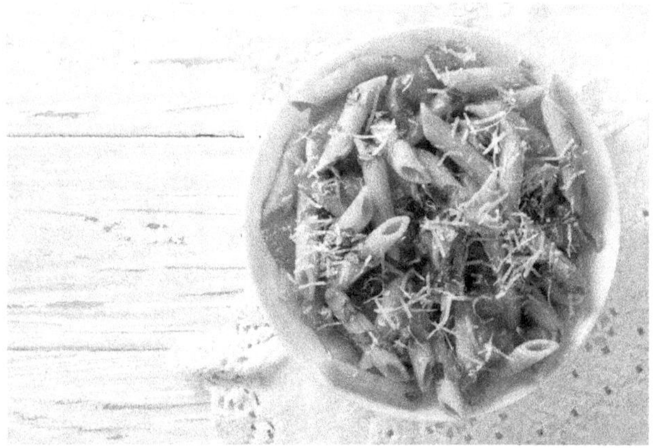

Ingredients:

- 300 g penne
- 2 red peppers
- 300 ml tomato passata
- some black olives
- 150 g smoked bacon cubes
- 100 g parmesan
- 30 basil leaves
- pepper & salt
- olive oil
- 4 garlic cloves

Preparation:

1. Cut the peppers and olives into pieces, peel the garlic and cook for 25 minutes in vacuum-sealable bags. Add the bacon cubes for the last 6 to 7 minutes.
2. Cook the penne al dente, drain and add the sauce. Add the tomato passata and simmer for another 5 minutes.
3. Season to taste, and add the parmesan and basil.

Spaghetti with cherry tomatoes and basil

Ingredients:

- 500g spaghetti
- 500g cherry tomatoes
- 2 ajuintjes
- 4 cloves of garlic
- A few basil leaves
- 2 tablespoons of olive oil
- 120 cl water
- Pepper and salt

Preparation:

1. Peel the onion and cloves and chop them. Wash the basil leaves and cut the cherry tomatoes in two or in four. Pour the water and olive oil into vacuum-sealable bags and add all other ingredients.
2. Bring to a boil over a high heat and cook for about 15 minutes. As soon as the cooking liquid is almost completely evaporated, you can serve and enjoy!

Cheesy chicken, broccoli and rice

Ingredients:

- 500g chicken fillet cut into small pieces
- 200g rice (extra long)
- 120g broccoli florets cut into pieces
- 100g chicken broth
- 200g grated cheddar
- 3 tablespoons olive oil
- 1 finely chopped onions
- 2 garlic cloves
- Salt and pepper

Preparation:

1. Stew the onion and garlic in olive oil in a large pan. Raise your fire and add the chicken that pre-season with salt and

pepper into vacuum-sealable bags. Wait a minute and then add the rice, the broth and the broccoli, put a lid on a separate vacuum-sealable bags and cook for about 20 minutes. When it's done, pour the cheese over the preparation. The only thing you still have to do is enjoy!

Pasta

This recipe costs little carving, so you have time for the nicer things in life. Below you will find all the ingredients and the preparation of the one pot of pasta.

Ingredients :

Preparation: 10 minutes

Cooking time: 10-15 minutes

- Dash of olive oil
- 4 cloves of garlic, finely chopped
- 2 red onions cut into thin rings
- 125 grams of mushrooms, in thin slices
- 500 ml vegetable stock
- 225 gram piece of cast
- 200 grams of bimi (baby broccoli) - or the florets of half a broccoli

- 350 grams of green asparagus, cut 1 cm from the hard bottom (may leave) and then into pieces of 3 cm
- 6 sundried tomatoes, in pieces
- 75 grams of grated Parmesan cheese
- Pepper and salt, to taste
- Chili flakes (optional)

Preparation:

2. Pour in some olive oil in a saucepan and fry the onion with the garlic and mushrooms for 2 minutes.
3. Add the vegetable stock, pasta, bimi, green asparagus and possibly some chili flakes and bring to the boil in a vacuum-sealable bags.
4. When it is completely cooking, set a timer to 8 minutes and stir the paste occasionally during this time in a bowl.
5. In a cooker, Turn off the heat after 8 minutes and add the Parmesan cheese and pieces of sundried tomato. Stir the ingredients for the one pot of pasta together and leave it on low heat for 2 minutes. Then switch off the fire.
6. Taste the pasta to taste and add some pepper and salt.
7. Divide this one-pan dish over two deep plates and the dish is read.

simple & delicious pasta dish

Ingredients:

- 1 tablespoon of olive oil
- 2 cloves of garlic, small cut
- 1 Spanish pepper, small cut
- 500 gram spaghetti
- 1200 ml water
- 250 grams sliced pieces of mushroom
- 1 courgette, in small cubes
- 3 hands of fresh spinach
- 200 grams of frozen peas
- 1 large tablespoon of thyme
- Pepper and salt
- A good blob of crème fraîche
- Noble yeast flakes (a kind of Parmesan-like taste)

Preparation:

1. Heat the olive oil in a large pan and fry the garlic and chilli pepper in 2 minutes.
2. Then place the rest of the ingredients, with the exception of the crème fraîche and the noble yeast flakes in the pan.

3. Bring the pasta to a boil, then reduce the heat and let it gently simmer for about 10 minutes, until the spaghetti is cooked. Stir the pasta occasionally.
4. Turn off the heat as soon as the spaghetti is done and drizzle the pasta with salt and pepper and add the crème fraîche and noble yeast flakes of your choice.
5. This one pot of pasta is the perfect healthy fast food meal after a long working day. Cycling to the snack bar takes more time. That extra kilo off sports, by the way.

Pasta

Ingredients (for 2-3 persons):

- 225-300 gr spaghetti
- 3 tomatoes
- 1 zucchini
- 1 (red) onion
- 1-2 red pepper (s)
- 2-3 cloves of garlic
- handful of cherry tomatoes
- large shoot tomato puree or passata
- Dash olive oil season
- To taste (use pepper, salt, oregano & paprika)

- Parmesan cheese (optional)
- water (+ stock cube)

Preparation:

1. Cut the vegetables to be cut into cubes.
2. Put all ingredients in a bag. Add a stock cube and bring it to the boil in vacuum-sealable bags. Then turn the heat a bit lower and let it simmer.
3. Boil the pasta in 10-14 minutes - depending on how you want it to be cooked or until the cooking liquid has thickened well.
4. Take out the pan from the heat, stir everything and scoop.
5. Serve to taste with grated Parmesan cheese. Simulator is almost impossible, right? You can vary with lots of vegetables, pasta types and even meat if you want this (of course you first fry this in the pan before adding the rest of the ingredients). Enjoy your meal!

Pepper stew with sausages

In this pepper stew it is at least delicious. It gives every tomato sauce or pepper recipe dish a big boost. It is the smoked taste and smell that creates a very fine Mediterranean taste.

Ingredients for 4 people

- 4 chipolata sausages
- kg peppers, in different colors (these are about 4 peppers + 3 pointed peppers)
- 2 onions
- 2 garlic cloves
- 125 gr crème fraîche
- 2 cans of tomatoes (à 400 gr)
- 2 tsp pimenton
- 4 sprigs fresh flat parsley
- Pepper and salt
- Olive oil

Preparation:

2. Remove the seed lists from the peppers. Cut them into long strips. Slice the onions and cloves of garlic.
3. Heat 3 tbsp olive oil in a casserole. Add the sausages into vacuum-sealable bags around brown. Remove them and set aside for a while.
4. Add the onions and garlic into vacuum-sealable bags. Spoon the peppers through. Put the tomato cubes in the pan. Add the pimenton with the paprika and tomato mixture. Put the sausages between the peppers.
5. Turn down the heat and then let it simmer for 45 minutes with the lid on the pan.
6. Season the pepper stew with the salt and freshly ground pepper from the grinder. Chop the parsley roughly. Sprinkle the pepper stew with the parsley and serve with a generous tablespoon of crème fraîche.

Mussels

Ingredients for 4 persons

- 3 kilos of mussels from Bart
- 1 onion
- 2 cloves garlic
- 200 gr cherry tomatoes
- Juice of 1 lemon
- Hand parsley
- Pepper and salt
- Olive oil

Preparation:

1. Start by checking the mussels. Rinse them under the tap and remove broken and open shells. These are not good and you have to throw away.
2. Peel and chop the onion and finely chop the garlic.
3. Take a large baking dish and distribute generous olive oil. Add the chopped onion and garlic and the mussels.
4. Add the cherry tomatoes and mix well together. Season with salt and pepper. The best thing is if you have a layer of mussels with enough space in between.

5. Cover the dish with aluminum foil, in this way steam the mussels steamed.
6. Put the mussels in the Instant Pot and steam them for 10 to 15 minutes. The more the mussels are distributed over the surface, the sooner they are ready. They are ready when the shells are nicely open.
7. Remove the mussels from the Instant Pot and sprinkle the lemon juice over them.
8. Garnish the mussels with some finely chopped parsley.
9. Serve with fries and or salad.

Tomato risotto with burrata

Ingredients for 4 people:

- 1 onion
- 1 garlic clove
- 300 gr risotto rice
- 1 dl white wine
- 400 gr tomatoes (tin)
- 400 ml (chicken) broth
- 40 gr Parmesan
- 1 bulb burrata
- Handful basil
- Pepper and salt

- Olive oil

Preparation:

1. Peel and chop the onion and finely chop a clove of garlic.
2. Fry this on a low heat in a little olive oil until the onion is glassy. Add the tomatoes and fry them.
3. Raise the fire slightly and add the risotto rice. Stir the whole for 2 minutes until the grains are translucent. Extinguish the mixture with the white wine and keep stirring until all the moisture has been absorbed.
4. Now add a little to the warm stock. Spoon a soup ladle of broth to the rice, keep stirring and wait until the moisture is absorbed. Repeat this step until all the broth has been absorbed.
5. Grate the Parmesan over the tomato risotto and season with salt and pepper.
6. The risotto is ready when it is al dente and smooth. The risotto must be liquid and "run" on the spoon.
7. Divide the tomato risotto over 4 plates. Garnish each plate with a portion of the burrata and finish with some fresh basil.
8. You can use the sous vade system, Place them in the vacuum-sealable bags and pour into the bags.
9. Prepare sous vide immersion circulator for use according to the manufacturer's directions. Preheat at water to 126°F (52°C).
10. Put the bags in the circulating water then cook it for 30 minutes for medium doneness.
11. Remove the bags from circulating water. Remove the menu from the bags and put them to dry.
12. Serve immediately.

Green couscous with feta

Ingredients for 4 people:

- 200 gr couscous
- 400 ml vegetable broth
- 3 spring onions
- 200 g peas
- 150 gr chickpeas
- 80 gr feta
- 40 gr pistachios
- Juice of half a lemon
- Hand of parsley
- Hand of fresh mint
- Pepper and salt
- Olive oil

Preparation:

1. Put the couscous inside a bowl and pour the hot stock on it. Add other ingredients into a bowl and mix. Place them in the vacuum-sealable bags and pour into the bags.
2. Prepare sous vide immersion circulator for use according to the manufacturer's directions. Preheat at water to 126°F (52°C).

3. Put the bags in the circulating water then cook it for 30 minutes for medium doneness.
4. Remove the bags from circulating water. Remove the menu from the bags and put them to dry.
5. Season with a dash of olive oil, the juice of half a lemon and some pepper and possibly a little salt.
6. Add the garden peas to the couscous.
7. Cut the spring onion into rings and finely chop the green herbs. Add this to the couscous.
8. Chop the pistachio nuts coarsely and add this together with the chickpeas to the rest. Cover well.
9. Garnish the green couscous with some feta and serve immediately.

Pot Gnocchi with lemon sauce and spinach

Ingredients for 4 people:

- 600 g gnocchi
- 500 g spinach
- 1 onion
- 2 cloves garlic
- 250 ml cream

- Juice and grater half a bio lemon
- 40 gr Parmesan
- Pepper and salt
- Olive oil

Preparation:

1. Peel and chop the onion and finely chop the garlic. Fry this in a large wok pan in a little olive oil.
2. Add the gnocchi and some extra olive oil and fry it all around. The gnocchi is ready if it has a nice crispy crust. Remove the gnocchi from the pan and keep them for later.
3. Now add the spinach little by little. Wok this shortly until all spinach has shrunk.
4. Extinguish the spinach with the cream and put the gnocchi back in the pan.
5. Season the cream sauce with salt and pepper and the juice and the grater of half a lemon. Stir everything briefly.
6. Add quite a bit of Parmesan and serve the one-pot gnocchi straight away.

Spring onion soup

Ingredients for 4 persons:

- 6 spring onions
- 750 ml cold (chicken) broth
- 1 garlic clove
- 30 gr butter
- 40 gr flour
- Sprig of parsley
- Spit cream
- Pepper and salt

Preparation:

1. Finely chop the garlic and cut the spring onions in rings.
2. Fruit them in the butter. Keep some of the spring onion behind for the garnish.
3. Add the flour and Peel and chop the onion and finely chop the garlic. Fry this in a large wok pan in a little olive oil.
4. Add the gnocchi and some extra olive oil and fry it all around. The gnocchi is ready if it has a nice crispy crust. Remove the gnocchi from the pan and keep them for later.
5. Now add the spinach little by little. Wok this shortly until all spinach has shrunk.
6. Extinguish the spinach with the cream and put the gnocchi back in the pan.
7. Season the cream sauce with salt and pepper and the juice and the grater of half a lemon. Stir everything briefly.
8. Let the spring onion soup simmer for a minute or 15 minutes. Puree the soup with a hand blender. Do you think the soup is too thick? add some extra broth.
9. Season the spring onion with pepper and salt.
10. Garnish the soup with some finely chopped parsley, a dash of cream and a few rings of spring onion. Serve immediately.

Gamba pan

Ingredients for 4 persons:

- 800 g prawns
- 1 onion
- 2 spring onions
- 2 cloves of garlic
- 0.5 red pepper
- 250 ml cream
- Juice of half a lemon
- Hand of parsley
- Pepper and salt
- Olive oil

Preparation:

- Clean the prawns or ask your fishmonger. Peel and chop the onion and finely chop the garlic and the red pepper (without seeds). Fruit this in something olive oil.
- Add the prawns Peel and chop the onion and finely chop the garlic. Fry this in a large wok pan in a little olive oil.

- Add the gnocchi and some extra olive oil and fry it all around. The gnocchi is ready if it has a nice crispy crust. Remove the gnocchi from the pan and keep them for later.
- Now add the spinach little by little. Wok this shortly until all spinach has shrunk.
- Extinguish the spinach with the cream and put the gnocchi back in the pan.
- Season the cream sauce with salt and pepper and the juice and the grater of half a lemon. Stir everything briefly..
- Add the cream and juice of half a lemon and let it boil slightly. If your gambas are pretty pink in color, they are done.
- Season the prawn pan with salt and pepper.
- Garnish the shrimp with spring onion sliced into rings and chopped parsley.
- Serve the gamba pan with bread. Of course, pasta or potatoes can also be used.

Wok dish with chicken and Asian pesto

Ingredients for 4 persons:

- 350 gr chicken thighs
- Pepper and salt
- 1 tbsp oil
- 20 gr butter
- 2 bunched onions, in rings
- 400 gr green beans
- 250 gr bean sprouts
- 300 gr broccoli, in florets
- 2 red peppers, in rings
- eggs
- 2 sprigs of fresh basil
- 2 sprigs of fresh coriander
- For the Asian pesto
- 2 tbsp sesame oil
- 1 tbsp soy sauce
- 90g unsalted peanuts
- 15g basil leaves
- 7g coriander leaves
- For the peanut sauce
- 1 tbsp honey
- 1 tbsp peanut butter
- 2 tsp lemon juice
- 1 tbsp sesame oil
- 1 tbsp balsamic vinegar
- 1 tbsp soy sauce

Preparation:

1. Prepare the pesto, put all ingredients for the Asian pesto in the chopper of the blender and grind to a paste. Set aside in a vacuum-sealable bags.
2. Make the peanut sauce. Put all ingredients for the peanut sauce in a bowl and stir well until a smooth sauce is created. Also put the peanut sauce vacuum-sealable bags aside.

3. Dab the chicken thighs dry with some paper towels. Sprinkle with salt and pepper. Take a large wok or large skillet. Add the butter and oil and Place them in the vacuum-sealable bags and pour into the bags.

4. Prepare sous vide immersion circulator for use according to the manufacturer's directions. Preheat at water to 126°F (52°C).

5. Put the bags in the circulating water then cook it for 30 minutes for medium doneness.

6. Remove the bags from circulating water. Remove the menu from the bags and put them to dry.

7. Put some oil in the pan and add the broccoli, green beans, spring onions and red pepper. Wok the vegetables until they get a color and are al dente, slide the vegetables aside and break the egg open in the pan. Hash the eggs through the pan so that the egg white and egg yolk coagulates. Put the bean sprouts in the pan. And scoop well.

8. Cut the chicken into strips and scoop them through the vegetables. Remove the pan from the heat. Put the peanut sauce in the pan and cover everything well. Divide the plates. Garnish with the pesto, fresh coriander and basil.

Pasta

Ingredients for two people:

- 150 grams of spaghetti
- 500 ml of water
- 1 vegetable stock cube
- 1 tin of tomato cubes (400 grams)
- 2 tablespoons of tomato paste
- 1 yellow pepper
- 1 onion
- 2 garlic cloves
- 1/4 t chilli flakes
- 1/2 tl of oregano
- 2 sprigs of basil

Preparation of the one pot of pasta:

1. Cut the onion into half rings; finely chop the garlic and the pepper into strips.
2. Remove the basil leaf from the twigs and cut the twigs. Keep the leaves separate for a while; you do not use them until the last time because otherwise the taste will boil out. Put all this in a pan with the rest of the ingredients.

3. Place them in the vacuum-sealable bags and pour into the bags.
4. Prepare sous vide immersion circulator for use according to the manufacturer's directions. Preheat at water to 126°F (52°C).
5. Put the bags in the circulating water then cook it for 30 minutes for medium doneness.
6. Remove the bags from circulating water. Remove the menu from the bags and put them to dry.
7. Cut the basil leaves coarsely and stir just before serving the pasta. If necessary, season the pasta with salt and pepper.
8. Serve in a deep plate, ready!
9. With this recipe you can vary considerably; use a different type of pasta, add zucchini or vega mince, serve with grated cheese or mozzarella. You can already hear it, the possibilities are endless. Enjoy your meal!

Rice

Ingredients for two people:

- 1 onion
- 2 garlic cloves
- 1 red pepper
- 1/2 tsp of smoked paprika
- 1/2 tsp curry powder

- Snuff cayenne pepper
- 400 grams of canned tomato cubes
- 300 ml of vegetable stock
- 200 grams of rice
- 175 grams of green beans
- 1 tomato cut into pieces
- Pepper and salt
- Sumac and / or lemon juice

Preparation:

1. Cut the onion and garlic fine. Cut the bell pepper into strips. Dop the beans and halve them.
2. Heat a little oil, onion and garlic. Then add the peppers and herbs (paprika, curry powder and cayenne pepper).
3. Add the rice, fry briefly and then add the tomatoes and stock.
4. Place them in the vacuum-sealable bags and pour into the bags.
5. Prepare sous vide immersion circulator for use according to the manufacturer's directions. Preheat at water to 126°F (52°C).
6. Put the bags in the circulating water then cook it for 30 minutes for medium doneness.
7. Remove the bags from circulating water. Remove the menu from the bags and put them to dry. After about 5 - 10 minutes you can add the green beans.
8. Taste if the rice is cooked, otherwise let stand with the lid on the pan. Turn the heat off then stir inside the wedges of tomato. Sprinkle some sumac over it and / or lemon juice.
9. If you have made too much, you can warm up the next day in the pan and eat it as lunch. Even tasted even better!

Chicken with beans and chickpeas

Light and tasty chicken with lots of juice and power. We make the chicken as a cooking pot, all the ingredients come into the pot at the same time and stand and simmer and adapt. Simple and comfortable.

Recipes for 4 people

Ingredients:

- 200 g red beans
- 200 g of chickpeas
- 1 tablespoon butter
- 1 tablespoon of olive oil
- 4 whole chicken thighs
- 1 teaspoon of herbal salt
- Pepper
- 2 shallots
- 2 sprigs of rosemary
- 250 g baby spinach
- 1 tomato without peel
- 1 cl of water

Preparation:

1. Place them in the vacuum-sealable bags and pour into the bags.
2. Prepare sous vide immersion circulator for use according to the manufacturer's directions. Preheat at water to 126°F (52°C).
3. Put the bags in the circulating water then cook it for 30 minutes for medium doneness.
4. Remove the bags from circulating water. Remove the menu from the bags and put them to dry.

A Mexican quinoa pot

Recipe for 4 people

- 3 peppers
- 3 roots
- 1 night spring onion
- 2 cloves of garlic
- 2 tablespoons of oil
- 1 letter taco spice (about 40 grams)
- 3 dl quinoa
- 1 kidney beans
- 2 chopped tomatoes

- 4 cups vegetable broth
- Sour cream
- Lime
- Fresh coriander

Preparation:

1. Wash very necessary ingredients and place them in the vacuum-sealable bags and pour into the bags.
2. Prepare sous vide immersion circulator for use according to the manufacturer's directions. Preheat at water to 126°F (52°C).
3. Put the bags in the circulating water then cook it for 30 minutes for medium doneness.
4. Remove the bags from circulating water. Remove the menu from the bags and put them to dry.

Lasagna soup - delicious soup with minced meat and pasta

In this delicious lasagne soup with minced meat and pasta you get all the delicious flavors of a traditional lasagna - this variety is much easier to prepare. The soup is smoked hot with small pieces of cheese.

Ingredients for 4 people:

- 2 roots

- 2 stalks of celery
- 1 onion (large)
- Olive oil
- 3 garlic cloves
- 500 g ground beef
- 1 tablespoon of thyme
- 2 teaspoons of rosemary
- Vegetable broth
- 2 ds of chopped tomatoes
- 1/2 of sun-dried tomatoes
- Salt
- Pepper
- 120 g macaroni
- 50 g Parmesan cheese
- 1 liter of basil
- 1 scoop mozzarella

Preparation:

1. Peel those carrots and cut into small cubes. Rinse celery and cut into small cubes. Move the onion and cut it into pieces.
2. Wrap the vegetables in olive oil in a vacuum medium heat. Finely chop the garlic and add to the vegetables. Let it bake until the onions are clear. You do not have to be brown.
3. Slide the vegetables to the edge of the pan and add the minced meat. Turn on the vacuum and burn the meat well. Add thyme, rosemary, vegetable broth, chopped tomatoes and dried tomatoes. Boil the soup and about 10 minutes
4. Taste the soup with salt and pepper, but be careful not to salt too much salt as it will require Parmesan cheese and salt later on.
5. Put the macaroni to the soup and cook for about 5 minutes until you are already dente. Stir in the Parmesan cheese,

break the basil leaves into smaller pieces and add. Refresh yourself with salt and pepper.

6. Serve.
7. Cut the mozzarella into small cubes. When serving, take a few cubes in the hot lasagna soup so they can melt in the soup.

Potato-Leek Soup

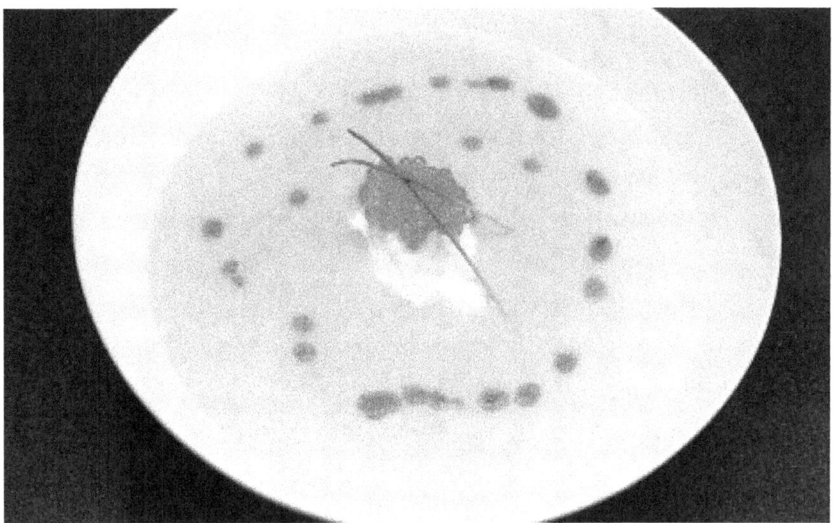

A classic potato soup does not have to be boring. This gives a good basic taste of chicken and white wine, a creamy consistency of the cream, while chives and caviar give the expression a stylish touch.

Recipe for 2 persons:

- 2 onions
- 3 leeks
- 2 tablespoons butter
- 300 g of potatoes
- 8 dl chicken broth or other broth or broth
- 2 dl white wine
- 2 dl cooking cream
- Chive oil

- 1 piece chives
- 2 dl rapeseed oil or other tasteless oil
- Garnish possible
- Sour cream
- Trout roe (or caviar)
- Chives

Preparation:

1. Chop the onions and cut the leek roughly. Sweat them in the butter in a pan. You should not get brown.
2. Peel potatoes and dice. Put the cubes in the vacuum and let them soak for half a minute before adding the broth and white wine.
3. Let the soup cook under the lid of the potatoes and the leek is soft (about 10 minutes). Meanwhile, the chive oil is produced.
4. Stir chives and oil together in a blender or mini-chopper until smooth.
5. Remove the pot of mashed potatoes from the heat and mix with a hand blender. Put the pan back on the heat and bring the soup to a boil. Add the cream and season with salt and pepper.
6. Serve soup with chive oil and possibly. a heap of sour cream and a spoonful of fresh trout, venison or caviar. Decorate the chives with a few stems.

Cod soup

The recipe for cod soup is a good main course for 2 people or a starter for 4 people.

- 2 people
- 2 shallots
- 2 tablespoons butter
- 1/2 fennel
- 6 dl fish box
- 2 1/2 dl cooking cream
- Salt
- Pepper
- 250 g cod fillet
- Watercress or other spice for decoration

Preparation:

1. Finely chop the shallots and fry in butter in vacuum. Cut the fennel into thin strips and add.
2. Pour the fish dish into the vacuum and bring the soup to a boil. Add the cooking cream with stirring. Season with salt and pepper.
3. Rinse cod fillets and cut into smaller pieces. Put it in the vacuum and let it simmer for a few minutes before you remove it from the heat and serve the cod soup.
4. Decorate with watercress, dill or other herb.

Beetroot soup

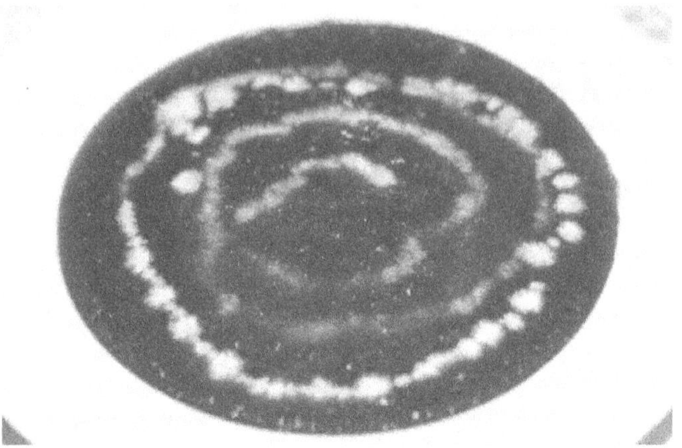

Beetroot soup is in some ways not boring. This gives a strong taste of beets, onions and broth. The color is (clear!) Not boring, but a nice, deep, red color. It also has a lot to offer as the beetroot is rich in iron, vitamin C and minerals.

For 4 people:

- 2 tablespoons olive oil
- 2 onions
- 2 cloves of garlic
- 6 turnips
- 5 cups beef broth
- Salt
- Pepper
- Some cream or creme fraiche

Preparation:

1. Finely chop onions and garlic. Sweat them in oil in a pan. Peel beetroot and cut into small pieces. Put them in the vacuum. Sweets take a minute before adding the beef buoy.
2. Bring the beetroot soup to a boil and cover. Bake the soup for 20 minutes or until the turnips are soft.

3. Mix the soup and pour it back into the pan. Season with salt and pepper and heat the soup well before serving.
4. When the beetroot soup is poured into the plates, it can be garnished / decorated with cream or dumpling cream.

Mexican stew with chicken

This Mexican stew is filled with soft chicken pieces, kidney beans, tomatoes, onions and garlic. The whole delicacy is mixed with rice and topped with fresh spring onions and creamy avocado.

For 4 people

- 1 onion
- 1 clove of garlic
- 2 tablespoons of oil
- 600 grams of chicken
- 1 red pepper
- 2 dl of rice
- 4 cups chicken broth
- 1 kidney beans
- 1 chopped tomato
- possibly 2 cups of corn
- 1 teaspoon of cumin
- possible. 1 teaspoon of chilli powder
- Salt
- Pepper
- 4 tomatoes

- 1 night spring onion
- 2 avocados
- a bit of lime juice or lemon juice
- 100 grams of grated cheddar cheese
- sour cream

Preparation:

1. Finely chop the onion and garlic.
2. Cut the chicken into a slice.
3. Cut the pepper into small cubes.
4. Add the chicken stock. Pour the alcohol from the kidney beans and add them together with the chopped tomatoes. May add the caraway and possibly. chili
5. Leave the bowl for about 15 minutes or until the rice is ready.
6. In the meantime the refilling is finished. Cut the tomatoes in half, remove soft grains and cut "tomato meat" into small cubes. Finely chop the spring onions.
7. Cut the avocados lengthwise, remove the stones and remove the green pulp with a spoon. Add cubes and lime juice or lemon juice. Taste the dish with salt and pepper and serve it with the topping.

Thai soup

Try Thailand with this Thai soup. It has the right aromas of ginger, curry paste and coconut milk. At the same time, the soup is doused with juicy chicken pieces, which also gives a nice snack. Can be served only as an aperitif or as a light meal.

Ingredients:

- 1 tablespoon of oil or butter
- 2 teaspoons of curry noodles
- 2 tablespoons of ginger
- 3 carrots
- 1 clove of garlic
- 1 onion (small)
- 2 bed spring onions
- 1 cl of water
- 250 g chicken
- 1 tablespoon chicken broth (concentrated)
- 3 dl coconut milk
- a little whipped cream for a creamier texture

Preparation:

1. Wipe the curry paste in a pan with the oil.
2. Peel ginger and one of the roots. Cookies garlic and onions. Cut off the top and the woody end of half of the spring onions. Cut everything into rough pieces and place it in the pan.
3. Sweat for a moment and then add the water. Put the chicken with the chicken broth in the pan. Simmer the Thai soup under the lid until the meat is cooked. Then pick up the meat and place it on a plate or something similar.
4. Pour the coconut milk into the soup and remove the pan from the heat. Mix the soup evenly with a hand blender.
5. Peel the last two roots and cut into thin strips, eg. For example, the last bunch of spring onions (do not forget to cut the top and the woody end first). Put the strips in the

pan and bring the soup to a boil. Slice the chicken and bring it in.

6. Add one. a little cream if you want a creamier consistency.

Fish in the bowl with coconut milk

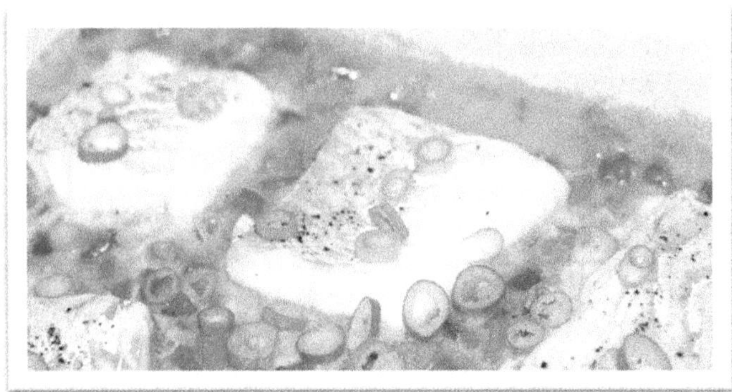

Really simple recipe for fish and vegetables in dishes with a creamy coconut milk sauce, mild red curry and a hint of lime.

Ingredients for 4 people:

- 400 g of carrots
- 2 tablespoons of oil
- 2 teaspoons of red curry paste (or "regular curry" to taste)
- 1 clove of garlic
- 4 peppers
- 1 ds of coconut milk
- Juice from 1 lime fruit
- salt
- Pepper
- 600 g of cod or other white fish
- 1 tablespoon of cornstarch or wheat flour for smoothing (can be easily omitted)
- 1 night spring onion

Preparation:

- Peel and cut carrots. Set vacuum-sealable bags and pour into the bags.
- Put the oil and wipe the curry paste (or normal curry) over medium heat. Put the carrots in vacuum-sealable bags and pour into the bags, let them cook for a few minutes while cutting the garlic and peppers. Stir in the carrots so they do not burn.
- Cut the garlic, cut into thin slices and place on the pan. Rinse the peppers, cut into cubes and place in the vacuum-sealable bags and pour into the bags. Take a few minutes to allow the peppers to add some liquid and small bites begin to soften.
- Add the coconut milk and cook over low heat. Try the coconut sauce with lime juice, salt and pepper. Even if necessary. Stir the sauce with cornmeal or wheat flour in a little cold water.
- Clean those spring onions, slice into slices and mix in the sauce (leave something to sprinkle the finished bowl).
- Clean the fish and dip it dry with a small paper towel or a clean dishcloth. Season with salt and pepper.
- Pour the coconut sauce into a pan and place the fish pieces on top. Stir the oven for about 12 minutes or until the fish is tender but still juicy.
- Sprinkle the last spring onions over it and eat the shell as it is.

Fischtopf

A fish pot that really delivers heat. The pot contains various ingredients that give a good taste. If you serve it with rice or potatoes, you can fill the dish even more.

Ingredients for 4 people:

- 500 g of cod
- 5 dl fish broth (heavy)
- 2 ½ dl cooking cream
- 2 peppers (possibly one red and one yellow)
- 2 red onions
- 2 leeks
- about 10 green asparagus
- 2 parsnips
- a little oil
- 1 pot of fresh dill
- salt
- pepper

Preparation:

1. Place them in the vacuum-sealable bags and pour into the bags.

2. Prepare sous vide immersion circulator for use according to the manufacturer's directions. Preheat at water to 126°F (52°C).
3. Put the bags in the circulating water then cook it for 30 minutes for medium doneness.
4. Remove the bags from circulating water. Remove the menu from the bags and put them to dry.
5. Serving suggestion: Pour the fish pot over brown rice or boiled potatoes and simmer the dish.

Fish soup

This excellent fish soup can be easily served as a meal during normal everyday life. It is a rich and satisfying soup with root vegetables as well as fish and shrimp, which gives a tasteful palette of taste and color. The chopped dill gives a fresh, green tone.

Ingredients for 4 people:

- 2 1/2 potatoes
- 2 carrots
- 1 parsnip
- 1 onion
- 2 tomatoes
- 1 teaspoon curry

- 1 teaspoon of oil
- 700 g white fish (eg sole or cod)
- 20 shrimp
- 2 storage cubes
- 9 dl of water
- 1 1/2 cooking cream
- 1 white wine
- salt
- pepper
- dill

Preparation:

1. Peel potatoes, carrots, parsnips and onions. Cut the first three into long pieces and cut them into small pieces. Season the vegetables with oil and curry. Mix well and add the tomatoes and custard cubes with water and white wine. Let it boil for 10 minutes before adding the flour.
2. Meanwhile, the fish are cut into medium sized pieces and the shrimp pills. Pour into the pan and simmer for 5 minutes over low heat. Season with salt and pepper. Add some chopped dill before serving.
3. Served with a good piece of bread.

Hot smoked salmon soup

Hot smoked salmon is something special in soups, but can also be replaced by almonds. Smoked salmon or maybe even fresh salmon. Remember that the fish must be frozen to avoid dangerous bacteria.

Ingredients for 2 people:

- 1 tablespoon butter
- 2 onions
- 4 fisheries funds
- 2 1/2 cooking cream (or milk - or a mixture)
- Salt
- White pepper
- 120 g warm smoked salmon
- Equipment
- Dill
- Pickled red onion

Preparation:

1. Place them in the vacuum-sealable bags and pour into the bags.
2. Prepare sous vide immersion circulator for use according to the manufacturer's directions. Preheat at water to 126°F (52°C).

3. Put the bags in the circulating water then cook it for 30 minutes for medium doneness.
4. Remove the bags from circulating water. Remove the menu from the bags and put them to dry.
5. Serve the warm soup with salmon pieces, red onions and dill.

Fish soup with leeks

Here, mild fishy taste is combined with leeks, one of the most popular ingredients in soups. Because of its good, but not ubiquitous flavor, it also delivers white wine, which adds additional flavors, sweet or sour, depending on the selected wine.

Decorate with oil drops and light green dill before serving to express a colorful game, and you have a nice gift, perfect for a dinner party.

Ingredients for 2 people

- 2 onions
- 2 tablespoons of oil
- 1 leek
- 8 dl fish stock or broth
- 2 dl white wine or sherry
- 250 g cod fillet
- 2 1/2 dl cooking cream

- Possible. 1 bld dill
- Salt
- Pepper
- Possible. a little oil for decoration

Direction:

1. Place them in the vacuum-sealable bags and pour into the bags.
2. Prepare sous vide immersion circulator for use according to the manufacturer's directions. Preheat at water to 126°F (52°C).
3. Put the bags in the circulating water then cook it for 30 minutes for medium doneness.
4. Remove the bags from circulating water. Remove the menu from the bags and put them to dry.

Thai fish soup

In the Thai fish soup the round fish taste is accompanied by slightly spicy and sour tones. Coconut milk gives a nice creamy consistency, while fresh vegetables and juicy pieces of fish make the soup a little bit rough.

Ingredients for 2 people:

- 1 tablespoon of oil

- 1 tablespoon curry paste
- 6 dl fish broth (or water + bouillon cube
- 1 tablespoon fish sauce
- 4 lime leaves
- 4 roots
- 100 g of green beans
- 1 night spring onion
- 2 cm ginger
- about 300 g of fish (eg cod)
- 1 ds of coconut milk
- Salt
- Pepper
- possible. fresh coriander

Direction:

1. Place them in the vacuum-sealable bags and pour into the bags.
2. Prepare sous vide immersion circulator for use according to the manufacturer's directions. Preheat at water to 126°F (52°C).
3. Put the bags in the circulating water then cook it for 30 minutes for medium doneness.
4. Remove the bags from circulating water. Remove the menu from the bags and put them to dry. Boil the fish soup briefly, season with salt and pepper and serve.
5. Decorate the Thai-inspired soup with fresh coriander to serve.

Lobster soup

Lobster is clearly used in soups. They have a fantastic taste of sea, salt and sweetness, combined in this soup with the taste of white wine, onions and peppers. And then it does not matter that it gets a nice, soft color.

Ingredients for 4 people:

- 2 tablespoons olive oil
- 2 tablespoons paprika powder
- 500 g lobster (or lobster tails, lobster tails, etc.)
- 3 dl white wine or sherry
- 3 dl of water
- 1 cube stock (eg fish, vegetable or chicken broth)
- 3 shallots or small almond onions
- 2 bay leaves
- 1 1/2 dl cream
- 1 sugar button
- Salt
- Pepper

Direction:

1. Cool the lobster candies from the bowls and keep them in the fridge.

2. Place them in the vacuum-sealable bags and pour into the bags.
3. Prepare sous vide immersion circulator for use according to the manufacturer's directions. Preheat at water to 126°F (52°C).
4. Put the bags in the circulating water then cook it for 30 minutes for medium doneness.
5. Remove the bags from circulating water. Remove the menu from the bags and put them to dry.

Simple tomato soup

This simple tomato soup is made from baked tomatoes, which makes them especially delicious and sweet. For example, the soup is served with crispy rye bread croutons and a bowl of fraiche.

Ingredients for 2 people:

- 1 kg of tomatoes (possibly on a stick)
- 1 red onion
- 3 garlic cloves
- 2 tablespoons of oil
- 2 teaspoons of thyme
- 2 teaspoons cane sugar
- 1 tablespoon creme fraiche 18%

- Salt
- Pepper
- Suggested accessories: rye bread croutons
- 3 slices of rye bread
- Oil
- •salt
- Portion
- Possible. Sour cream
- Possible. Fresh basil

Direction:

1. Put the tomatoes in a bowl - let the stems stand when using tomatoes on a stalk. Kiss red onions and garlic and cut into large pieces. Spread the onions and garlic over the tomatoes. Cover with oil and sprinkle with thyme and sugar. Cook the tomatoes for 1 hour at 160 degrees - you can bake them for a shorter time, but then increase the heat of the oven.
2. Remove the stems from the tomatoes and pour the entire contents of the bowl into a blender. You can also use a hand blender and simply put the contents in a pan. Mix the soup well, so that no lumps arise. Stir in the crème fraiche and season with salt and pepper. Serve soup immediately or heat in a pan.
3. Simple suggestions for accessories - rye bread croutons:
4. While the tomatoes are there, you can make rye bread croutons. Cut the rye bread into small cubes and place with baking paper on a vaccum. Pour over oil and sprinkle with salt. Bake the last 15 minutes of the tomato baking time in the oven. Let the croutons cool down.
5. Serve the tomato soup with the crispy rye bread croutons. an extra drop of sour cream and fresh basil.

Good tomato soup

One of the best tomato soup recipes you can get. After adding the delicious ingredients, cook the soup under the lid for 10 minutes. Serve hot.

Ingredients:

- 2 tablespoons olive oil
- 2 onions (big)
- 2 cloves of garlic
- 2 dl sherry or white wine
- 4 ds peeled tomatoes (or chopped tomatoes)
- 2 tablespoons chicken broth (or vegetable broth)
- 2 teaspoons of sugar
- Salt
- Pepper
- Krydderöl
- 2 pots of basil or parsley
- 3 dl olive oil
- Salt
- Pepper

Direction:

1. Chop onions and garlic and fry in oil (they must not take on any color). Add the tomatoes to sherry or white wine. Add one. Money to give the soup more abundance.
2. Simmer the soup under the lid for 10 minutes.
3. The spice oil is made while the soup is simmering in the vaccum. Mix basil leaves or parsley with oil, salt and pepper.
4. Season the soup with sugar, salt and pepper. Serve hot and dripping herbal oil.

Tomato Soup

In most supermarkets, you will receive a ready-made tomato soup. This solution is simple and inexpensive and is suitable for busy days or at the end of the month. The soup can be easily absorbed with milk, water and finally with a creamy sour cream surface.

Ingredients:

- 1 ds tomato soup (at 440 g)
- 2 1/2 dl of milk
- 2 dl of water
- 4 tablespoons creme fraiche

Direction:

1. The soup comes in a vacuum. Milk and water are added and cooked.
2. The soup is ready to serve and is best served with hugs and nice places.
3. Do not forget to do so with soups, on the packaging of which you can mix milk or cream.

103. Tacosuppe

This delicious taco soup is full of flavor and rich in proteins, vitamins and iron. Beef and kidney beans make it particularly satisfying, with a handful of crunchy Nacho cream and whipped cream.

Ingredients for 4 people:

- 2 onions (big)
- oil
- 2 cloves of garlic
- 2 ds chopped tomatoes
- 2 liters of water
- 1 block beef broth
- 2 ds tomatos puree (140 grams)
- 1 fresh chili
- 400 g minced meat (or minced pork and veal)
- a little oil

- 200 g kidney beans
- 1 ps taco spice
- 1 ds corn

Equipment:

- Grated cheese
- Sour cream
- Nachos

Direction:

1. Cut the onion well and fry in a vacuum bag in a little oil. Add garlic, add and sweat until the onions are golden. Add chopped tomatoes, water, stock and tomato puree and cook.
2. Wipe off the peppers, remove the grains and obstructions, and finely chop them. Then put it in the pan.
3. Mix the soup together using a hand blender until the desired consistency is achieved.
4. Beat the minced meat in small oil in a pan. Then add the kidney beans (without layer) and the taco spice. Mix well and add everything. Water if necessary.
5. Put meat and beans in the vacuum bag and add corn. Bring soup to boil and let it work for a few minutes. If the soup is too thick, you can. Add some water.
6. Serve the soup in a deep bowl of grated cheese, dumpling cream and a handful of nachos.

Tomato soup with noodles

Beautiful full tomato soup with small pieces of pasta that give a little extra filling. It's quick and easy to make and it's even healthy.

Ingredients for 3 people:

- 2 onions
- 1 tablespoon of oil
- 2 cloves of garlic
- 1/2 cup of white wine (or water)
- 2 ds chopped tomatoes
- 1 block chicken broth
- 1/2 l of water (boiling)
- 2 tablespoons fresh thyme (finely chopped)
- 80 g pasta (or spaghetti)
- Salt
- Pepper

Direction:

1. Cut the onions and sweat in a medium sized pan over medium heat. Crush the garlic and let it sweat. The onions are glassy.

2. Add white wine when the onions take on color. Let the alcohol evaporate and add the chopped tomatoes, broth, water and thyme.
3. Let the soup boil for 10-15 minutes.
4. Puree the pasta so that the pieces are a few inches long and add them. Cook the tomato soup until the pasta is ready and season with salt and pepper.
5. Tips:
6. You can easily use water instead of white wine if you do not like the taste. If you use water, it is advisable to add lemon juice.
7. The fresh thyme can also be replaced by dried thyme, but only half.

Pumpkin soup with shrimp

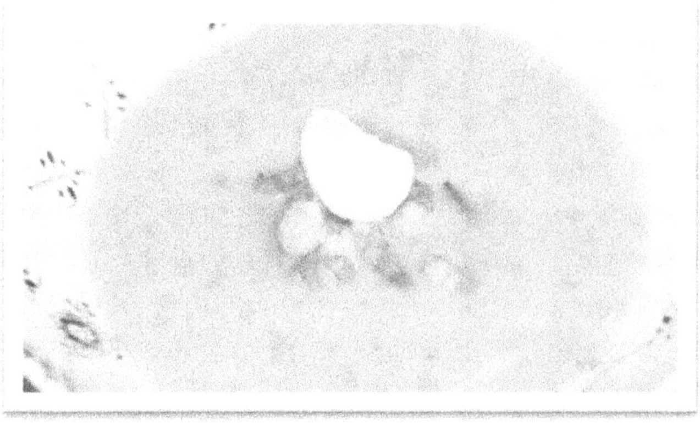

The taste of pumpkin soup depends very much on what type of pumpkin is used. Use Hokkaido or Buttercup Pumpkin for cooking. They are not the best pumpkins, but they taste the best.

The shrimp in the soup give it a bite, while saffron and lime give extra flavor. The soup can be part of a delicious meal as a tasty appetizer, but it can also be a crazy meal.

Ingredients for 3 people:

- 1 kg pumpkin
- 3 onions
- 1 clove of garlic
- 2 tablespoons butter
- 1 liter chicken broth
- Possible. 1 knaf of saffron
- 2 dl cooking cream (or milk - depending on the desired consistency / taste)
- Salt
- Pepper

Equipment:

- 300 g shrimp (drained weight)
- Sour cream
- Lime juice

Preparation:

1. Peel the carpet on the lawn and scrape off the seeds with a spoon. Cut the pumpkin meat into smaller pieces. Finely chop onions and garlic.
2. Put the onions, garlic and pumpkin pieces in a butter pan.
3. Add chicken stock and optional. Saffron Simmer the soup under the lid until the carcass pieces are soft.
4. Wash very necessary ingredients and place them in the vacuum-sealable bags and pour into the bags.
5. Prepare sous vide immersion circulator for use according to the manufacturer's directions. Preheat at water to 126°F (52°C).
6. Put the bags in the circulating water then cook it for 30 minutes for medium doneness.
7. Remove the bags from circulating water. Remove the menu from the bags and put them to dry.
8. Serve the hot pumpkin soup with shrimp, dumpling cream and lime juice drops.

Pumpkin soup with bacon and cream

This great pumpkin soup tastes great with garlic and rosemary. It has cream added and gives a nice creamy consistency, which is complemented by the crunchy bacon above. A real autumn soup.

Ingredients for 6 people:

- 1 Hokkaidograaf
- 140 g bacon
- 2 onions
- 2 cloves of garlic
- 2 cubed vegetable bouillon
- 3 sprigs of rosemary
- Water
- 1 1/2 cream
- Salt
- Pepper

Preparation:

1. Place them in the vacuum-sealable bags and pour into the bags.

2. Prepare sous vide immersion circulator for use according to the manufacturer's directions. Preheat at water to 126°F (52°C).
3. Put the bags in the circulating water then cook it for 30 minutes for medium doneness.
4. Remove the bags from circulating water. Remove the menu from the bags and put them to dry.
5. Fish the rosemary and mix the soup until it is completely creamy. Add cream, season with salt and pepper.
6. Serve the broth with the crispy bacon on it.

Indian vegetarian curry

Great vegetarian stew with chickpeas and excellent Indian flavor, made from sweet spices. The coconut milk makes the sauce creamy without dairy, the curry is even vegan.

Ingredients for 6 people:

- 5 cm ginger
- 2 onions (big)
- 4 cloves of garlic
- 1 red pepper
- 2 tablespoons olive oil

- 1 1 2 tablespoons Garam Masala
- 1 teaspoon of cumin
- 1 to 2 teaspoons of coriander
- 2 teaspoons turmeric
- 1 teaspoon of cayenne pepper (can be cut in half or omitted if you do not pay attention to strong food)
- 3 tablespoons tomato puree
- 2 ds chickpeas
- 1 ds chopped tomatoes
- 1 ds of coconut milk
- 2 1/2 dl vegetable broth
- Salt
- Pepper
- 50 g almonds
- 75g baby spinach
- Rice
- Naan bread
- Natural yogurt

Preparation:

1. Peel ginger, onions and garlic. Cut off the three things well - it can easily be done in a food processor.
2. Remove the white obstacles and seeds from the pepper and cut into cubes.
3. Place them in the vacuum-sealable bags and pour into the bags.
4. Prepare sous vide immersion circulator for use according to the manufacturer's directions. Preheat at water to 126°F (52°C).
5. Put the bags in the circulating water then cook it for 30 minutes for medium doneness.
6. Remove the bags from circulating water. Remove the menu from the bags and put them to dry.

7. Finely chop the almonds and rinse the baby spinach well. Add both to the pan and simmer for five minutes until the spinach collapses.
8. The delicious vegetarian curry with rice, naan bread and natural yoghurt, for example, makes for a complete Indian party.

Beef stew

Preparation time: 35 minutes

Total time: 50 minutes

Ingredients:

- 1 1/2 pounds of beef stew
- 1 tablespoon of olive oil
- 1 teaspoon salt
- 1 teaspoon of pepper
- 1 teaspoon Italian herbs
- 2 tablespoons of Worcestershire sauce
- 3 garlic cloves, chopped

- 1 large onion, chopped
- 1 16 bags of baby carrots, cut
- 1 pound of potatoes in cubes
- 2 1/2 cups of beef broth
- 1-2 tomato sauce
- 2 tablespoons cornmeal
- 2 tablespoons of water

Instructions:

1. Place them in the vacuum-sealable bags and pour into the bags.
2. Prepare sous vide immersion circulator for use according to the manufacturer's directions. Preheat at water to 126°F (52°C).
3. Put the bags in the circulating water then cook it for 30 minutes for medium doneness.
4. Remove the bags from circulating water. Remove the menu from the bags and put them to dry.
5. Mix flour and cold water in a small bowl and stir in the stew until thicker.

Nutrition:

- Calories: 384 kcal
- Carbohydrates: 23 g
- Protein: 42 g
- Fiber: 3 g
- Sugar: 2 g
- Vitamin A: 0.7%
- Vitamin C: 20.3%
- Calcium: 10.3%
- Iron: 45.4%

Beef stew

Preparation time 20 minutes

Cooking time 4 hours

Total time 4 hours and 20 minutes

Ingredients:

- 2 tablespoons olive oil
- 2 pounds of stew
- Salt and pepper to taste
- 2 tablespoons all-purpose flour
- 1 teaspoon dried thyme
- 2 teaspoons of smoked paprika
- 1 large onion, cube
- 3 garlic cloves, pressed
- 3 medium carrots, chopped

- 2 celery stalks, chopped
- 1/2 cup of red wine
- 2 strips of Worcestershire sauce
- 2 tablespoons of tomato puree
- 1/2 cup tomato sauce
- 3 cups low sodium beef
- 5 medium white potatoes, quartered
- 1 cup of frozen green beans (optional)
- Fresh parsley for garnish

Instructions:

1. Place them in the vacuum-sealable bags and pour into the bags.

2. Prepare sous vide immersion circulator for use according to the manufacturer's directions. Preheat at water to 126°F (52°C).
3. Put the bags in the circulating water then cook it for 30 minutes for medium doneness.
4. Remove the bags from circulating water. Remove the menu from the bags and put them to dry. You know that the stew is ready at the end of the set time and the pieces of meat disintegrate when you touch them with a fork.
5. Serve in deep bowls, add a piece of crispy bread and sprinkle with fresh parsley (if desired).

Stew Simple beef stew recipe

Ingredients:

- Cut 2.5 pounds of beef breast fat, cut meat into cubes of 1.5 to 2 inches
- crushed 1 carrot
- Dice 1 onion
- 2 tablespoons all-purpose flour
- 2 teaspoons kosher salt
- 1 teaspoon of black pepper
- 1 teaspoon of garlic powder
- 1/4 teaspoon cayenne pepper (optional)
- 1/2 teaspoon smoked paprika
- 1 teaspoon onion powder
- Liquids for beef stew
- 8 oz tomato sauce
- 1/4 cup of water (or broth / broth / red wine)

Instructions:

1. Place them in the vacuum-sealable bags and pour into the bags.

2. Prepare sous vide immersion circulator for use according to the manufacturer's directions. Preheat at water to 126°F (52°C).
3. Put the bags in the circulating water then cook it for 30 minutes for medium doneness.
4. Remove the bags from circulating water. Remove the menu from the bags and put them to dry. Add beef, herbs, water and tomato puree, stir, cover with lid and cook for 3 hours until everything is ready.

Perfect potato soup

Ingredients:

- 6 Russian potatoes, peeled and sliced
- 1/2 inch cubes
- Cut into 5 slices of bacon
- 1/2 inch pieces
- 3 tablespoons butter
- Cut 2 strips of celery into 1/4 inch slices
- 1/2 large onion, spicy small
- Cut 20 carrots into 1/4 inch pieces
- 2 teaspoons kosher salt, divided
- 1 1/2 teaspoons of freshly ground black pepper
- 3 tablespoons all-purpose flour

- 2 cups one and a half and a half
- 1 1/2 cups chicken broth
- 1/4 teaspoon dried thyme
- 1/8 teaspoon cayenne pepper
- 1 shot of peanuts
- 4 spring onions, finely chopped

Preparation time 30 minutes

Kitchen: 50 m

Ready in 1 hour 20 m

Preparation:

1. Place the ingredients in the vacuum-sealable bags and pour into the bags.
2. Prepare sous vide immersion circulator for use according to the manufacturer's directions. Preheat at water to 126°F (52°C).
3. Put the bags in the circulating water then cook it for 30 minutes for medium doneness.
4. Remove the bags from circulating water. Remove the menu from the bags and put them to dry.
5. Ladle in bowls. Garnish with 1/2 teaspoon of pepper, spring onions and peppers. Serve it
6. Nutritional information
7. Pr. Serving: 396 calories; 18.8 g fat; 47.6 g carbohydrates; 10.8 g protein; 55 mg cholesterol; 1165 mg of sodium. All food.

Bavarian potato soup

Preparation: 45 m

Cooking: 1 hour 3 m

Ready for 1 hour 48 m

Ingredients:

- 2 combined pork sausages
- 3 tablespoons of vegetable oil or to taste
- 4 pounds of potatoes, peeled and diced
- Dice 4 carrots
- 2 onions, finely chopped
- 1 leek, cut and diced
- 3 stallions, hacked
- 3 garlic cloves, chopped
- 1 cubic vegetable bouillon
- 6 cups of hot water
- 1 teaspoon of salt or to taste
- 1 teaspoon freshly ground black pepper or season to taste
- 1 pinch of dried marjoram or flavor
- 1 chili pepper or flavor
- 1 knife or taste
- 1 bunch of fresh parsley, minced meat

- 1 bunch of fresh piece, chopped
- 1/4 cup cream cream (optional)

Preparation:

1. Dissolve the vegetable stock in hot water and pour into the pot.
2. Season the soup with salt, black pepper, marjoram, paprika and nutmeg. Place the ingredients in the vacuum-sealable bags and pour into the bags.
3. Prepare sous vide immersion circulator for use according to the manufacturer's directions. Preheat at water to 126°F (52°C).
4. Put the bags in the circulating water then cook it for 30 minutes for medium doneness.
5. Remove the bags from circulating water. Remove the menu from the bags and put them to dry. Cooking Reduce the heat to low and cook until the carrots are soft (about 30 minutes).
6. Stir fried sausage, parsley and steaks in the soup. Spread until the aromas stir in sour cream about 5 minutes before serving.

Potato Broccoli Cheese Soup

Ingredients:

- 2 cups of chopped onions
- 2 tablespoons margarine
- 2 1/2 pounds of peeled and diced potatoes
- 5 cups of boiling water
- 4 cubes of chicken broth
- 3 cups fresh broccoli cooked and dehydrated salt and pepper to taste
- 3 cups of grated cheddar cheese

Preparation:

1. Place them in the vacuum-sealable bags and pour into the bags.
2. Prepare sous vide immersion circulator for use according to the manufacturer's directions. Preheat at water to 126°F (52°C).
3. Put the bags in the circulating water then cook it for 30 minutes for medium doneness.
4. Remove the bags from circulating water. Remove the menu from the bags and put them to dry. Add half of the soup to the blender or food processor in the storage container. Season with salt and pepper.
5. Add cheese and heat soup until the cheese has melted. Server is called

Chicken soup with cheese and broccoli

Ingredients:

- 1/2 cup butter
- 1 cup of flour
- 11 cups of water
- Chicken broth with 3 cubes
- 2 pounds without skin, boneless halves of chicken fillet - each cut into pieces
- Fresh broccoli with 2 cups, cut into flowers
- 1 1/2 teaspoons salt
- 1 teaspoon black black pepper
- 1 cup of light cream
- 3 cups of grated cheddar cheese
- Preparation: 10 m
- Cooking: 1 hour

Preparation:

1. Distribute the butter over medium heat in a 5 liter pan. Stir the flour with constant stirring until a thick paste is formed. Remove from the pan and set aside.

1. Place them in the vacuum-sealable bags and pour into the bags.
2. Prepare sous vide immersion circulator for use according to the manufacturer's directions. Preheat at water to 126°F (52°C).
3. Put the bags in the circulating water then cook it for 30 minutes for medium doneness.
4. Remove the bags from circulating water. Remove the menu from the bags and put them to dry.

Nutritional Information:

- 434 calories
- 26.6 g fat
- 15.3 carbohydrates
- 33.4 g protein
- 129 mg cholesterol
- 1059 mg of sodium.

Northern Italian beef stew

Preparation: 30 m

Cooking: 4 hours 20 m

Ready for 4 hours 50 m

Ingredients:

- 2 tablespoons olive oil
- 2 pounds of lean buds, cut and cut into 1-inch cubes
- 2 large sweet onions, cubes
- 2 cups of celery
- 4 large carrots, peeled, cut into large circles
- 1 pound Crimini mushrooms, slices
- 2 tablespoons chopped garlic
- 2 cups of dry red wine
- 4 big tomatoes, chopped
- 1 1/2 pounds of red potatoes (like red bliss), cut into 1-inch pieces
- 1 tablespoon of dried basil
- 1 teaspoon dried thyme
- 1 teaspoon dried marjoram
- 1/2 teaspoon dried sage
- 1 quartz beer
- 2 cups tomato sauce

Preparation:

1. Heat the olive oil inside a large saucepan over medium heat. Cook the steak in hot oil until it is completely brown. About 5 minutes per batch. Remove the brown cube for a dish covered with paper towels, leave the casserole warm and let the meat drain.
2. Place them in the vacuum-sealable bags and pour into the bags.
3. Prepare sous vide immersion circulator for use according to the manufacturer's directions. Preheat at water to 126°F (52°C).
4. Put the bags in the circulating water then cook it for 30 minutes for medium doneness.

5. Remove the bags from circulating water. Remove the menu from the bags and put them to dry.

Potato cheddar soup

Ingredients:

- 2 cups of water
- 2 cups peeled and diced red potatoes
- 3 tablespoons of melted butter
- 1 small onion, chopped
- Season 3 tablespoons of salt and pepper
- 3 cups of milk
- 1/2 teaspoon white sugar
- 1 cup of grated cheddar cheese
- 1 cup of ham

Preparation:

1. Boil water inside a medium saucepan, add the potatoes and cook until tender. Drain reserves a cup of liquid.
2. Stir in butter, onions and flour. Season with salt and pepper. Slowly stir in the potatoes, liquid, milk, sugar, cheese and ham. Lubricate for 30 minutes and stir regularly.

Nutritional information:

- Calories
- g fat
- 12.3 g carbohydrates
- g protein
- 34 mg cholesterol
- 277 mg of sodium

Chickpea Stew and Swiss Chard

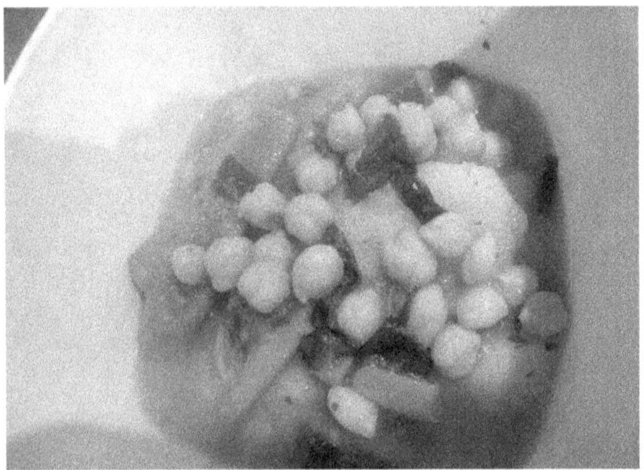

Ingredients:

Four servings

For chickpeas:

- 300grs chickpeas butter
- One onion
- Two garlic cloves
- One laurel leaf
- Salt
- For the sofrito:
- One onion
- ½ leek
- Two cloves garlic

- One tomato
- One piece red pepper
- One piece of green pepper
- One cdita sweet paprika
- Salt
- extra virgin olive oil
- Other ingredients:
- ¼kg Swiss chard or spinach
- Two potatoes waterfalls
- Two carrots in pieces
- 1/4 kg green beans
- Two boiled eggs

Preparation

30 minutes

1. Put to soak the chickpeas with a pinch of baking soda, salt, Place them in the vacuum-sealable bags and pour into the bags.
2. Prepare sous vide immersion circulator for use according to the manufacturer's directions. Preheat at water to 126°F (52°C).
3. Put the bags in the circulating water then cook it for 30 minutes for medium doneness.
4. Remove the bags from circulating water. Remove the menu from the bags and put them to dry. Serve with a hardboiled egg cut in half.

A Stew Of Beef

Ingredients:

Four servings

- 500grs carrots
- 750grs beef to stew (you tell the butcher you want Morcillo or needle)
- Two laurel leaves
- One onion
- One garlic head
- 1/3 glass wine rancid
- 100 gr tomato
- Water
- oil and salt
- Colorant

Preparation:

75 minutes

1. Place them in the vacuum-sealable bags and pour into the bags.

2. Prepare sous vide immersion circulator for use according to the manufacturer's directions. Preheat at water to 126°F (52°C).
3. Put the bags in the circulating water then cook it for 30 minutes for medium doneness.
4. Remove the bags from circulating water. Remove menu from the bags and pat dry and serve.

Ox Or Beef Tail

Ingredients:

Four servings

- 1Kg. oxtail I do it veal
- Two large onions
- Two carrots
- Two ripe tomatoes
- Three cloves garlic
- Some saffron threads
- Salt and pepper
- 1/2 liter wine from Montilla or a good black wine. (no water or broth is added to it, it is cooked only with wine)

- 50 gr oil

Preparation:

30 minutes

1. Place them in the vacuum-sealable bags and pour into the bags.
2. Prepare sous vide immersion circulator for use according to the manufacturer's directions. Preheat at water to 126°F (52°C).
3. Put the bags in the circulating water then cook it for 30 minutes for medium doneness.
4. Remove the bags from circulating water. Remove the menu from the bags and put them to dry. It can be accompanied with good fries.

Preparations:

• Once cut the morrón, the onion, and the peeled and diced potatoes, previously cooked. Mix everything in a pot. Add a tablespoon of vegetable oil, add the onion and the full nose. Let it cook a little, add the seasonings to the see that it gets thick. Stir the glass of hot water. Once all previously prepared add the sliced green onion and the chopped egg plus the previously cooked potatoes. The patty is already cooked. In the end, put the tripe cut.

• The tripe clarify that it is well cut into squares and ready

• Put in a pot that uses the entire fat heat well, and that's it. Eye before you burn it to mix it and take it with oil. The tic is that the first dozen are spectacular and those that remain delicious.

• Step echo fills the place with the love of food and tradition. Thanks for making the recipe.

Chicken And Mine (Bartolo)

Ingredients:

Three servings

- Four chicken legs (in this case)
- Four carrots
- 4 to 6 potatoes
- 3 to 4 onions
- One garlic melon
- One morrón of color to choose
- One dl orange lentils
- One good touch of oil
- One recontra touch of curry
- One right touch of coarse salt
- One pressure cooker when there is little time or.
- One ordinary saucepan when there is time.

Preparations:

30 minutes

1. Cut the carrots into truncated cylinders or cones of 3-4cm and then to the middle transversely and if they are thick,

cross them again into four sections. Give the potatoes without peeling them after brushing them under water.

2. Peel and cut the thick onions.
3. Mess with the morrón
4. Place them in the vacuum-sealable bags and pour into the bags.
5. Prepare sous vide immersion circulator for use according to the manufacturer's directions. Preheat at water to 126°F (52°C).
6. Put the bags in the circulating water then cook it for 30 minutes for medium doneness.
7. Remove the bags from circulating water. Remove the menu from the bags and put them to dry.

Vegetables "Garnish For the Diet."

Ingredients:

Four servings

- Two onions girls
- One carrot
- 1/2 red bell
- One eggplant

- Two slices squash anco
- One big green zucchini or 2 kids
- Salt and pepper
- Seeds to sprinkle (optional)

Preparations:

20 minutes

1. Cut the vegetables into large sizes. Place inside the sous vide vaccum with 1 tbsp. oil
2. Salt and pepper to taste. Cover it, and then cook according to the time indicated by the sous vide vaccum. In case you do it in the common pot cover and let cook over low heat until tender.
3. Serve warm accompanied by some lean churrasquito or breast.

Potato And Vegetable Pan With Beluga Lentils

Try this is a down-to-earth dish with a modern twist.

Preparation: 10 minutes

Cooking time: 25 minutes

Total time: 35 minutes

Ingredients:

- 100 g (1/2 cup) Beluga lentils
- 250 ml (1 cup) of water
- 2-3 tbsps. Olive oil
- Three carrots
- Two potatoes
- One sweet potato
- 50 g wild garlic butter
- 1/2 teaspoon salt
- 1/4 tsp. pepper (optional)
- 1/4 tsp. paprika, sweet
- 1 tbsp. fresh chopped parsley (optional)

Preparation:

1. Place them in the vacuum-sealable bags and pour into the bags.
2. Prepare sous vide immersion circulator for use according to the manufacturer's directions. Preheat at water to 126°F (52°C).
3. Put the bags in the circulating water then cook it for 30 minutes for medium doneness.
4. Remove the bags from circulating water. Remove the menu from the bags and put them to dry.

HINTS:

- Alternatively, garlic butter, herb butter or plain butter can be used in combination with two finely chopped garlic cloves.

Pickled Chicken

This pot takes me out of a thousand troubles! And for the summer the pickle is ideal.

Ingredients:

Six servings

- One chicken without skin and bone
- One tacit oil
- One unspoiled vinegar
- 1/2 white glass wine
- One lemon sliced
- Two carrots julienne
- Two cloves garlic
- Two sliced onions
- Salt and pepper

Preparation:

1. Cut and bone the chicken. Brown lightly and reserve.
2. Then sauté the vegetables in the vacuum-sealable bags. Add chicken prey and other ingredients. Cover and cook 15 minutes.

Goulash

Ingredients:

- • 600 g   beef goulash
- 1 m. Large Carrot (n)
- 1 m. Large Potato (n)
- 2 Spring onions)
- 1 tbsps. Tomato paste
- 100 ml Red wine, dry
- 500 ml of vegetable stock
- 2 Teaspoons Pimento de la Vera
- One teaspoon Paprika powder, rosy or mild to taste
- salt
- Pepper, black
- 5 tbsps. Milk
- 2 TL heaped   food starch

Preparation:

Working time: approx. 40 min

1. Peel the carrot and the potato and, together with the spring onions, finely grate into mush or grind into pulp in the shredder. The vegetable musk gives a good sauce base without bits and passing.

2. Fry the goulash in the sous vide vaccum, add the vegetable nutmeat and the tomato paste and sauté as well. It may start quietly. Deglaze with the red wine, solve the gravy and bring the red wine to a boil. Stir in the spices and add the broth.
3. Close the lid and set the print time to 20 minutes.
4. You can, either open the steam valve. Open the lid, mix the milk with the starch and stir in and boil again for 5 minutes, so that the sauce is beautifully creamy and sets. Finally, to taste still.
5. Spätzle, rice or dumplings are a perfect match.
6. Tip: If you omit the corn flour, you will get a delicious goulash soup.

Pea Soup

Ingredients 4 servings

- A tablespoon-free butter
- A tablespoon of extra virgin olive oil
- A medium onion, chopped
- A stalk of celery, chopped
- Two garlic cloves, chopped
- A teaspoon of chopped fresh thyme or parsley

- Six cups of peas, fresh or frozen
- ½ cup of water
- 4 cups for chicken broth with reduced sodium quality, broth without vegetables or vegetable broth
- ½ cup fifty (optional)
- ½ teaspoon salt freshly ground pepper.

Preparations:

Preparation time 35m:

1. Heat the butter and oil in an oven over medium heat until the butter melts. Add onions and celery; Cook, stir until soft, 4 to 6 minutes.
2. Add garlic with thyme (or parsley); Boil, stir until it smells, about 10 seconds. Stir peas
3. Add water and broth; Bring it to a lively boil over high heat. Reduce the heat to maintain cooking and cook until tender. 1 minute Purée the soup in batches in a blender. (Be careful when reading hot liquids.) Mix half and half (if used), salt and pepper.

Pumpkin and Apple Soup

Ingredients:

- 450 g pumpkin
- 1 Granny Smith apple seed and quince
- A medium onion is cut
- Two garlic cloves
- One tablespoon of olive oil
- salt
- ¼ teaspoon cayenne pepper more to taste
- 300 ml vegetable broth
- freshly ground black pepper for seasoning

Garnish:

- Pomegranate Arillen
- some pumpkin seeds
- finely chopped fresh parsley

The preparations:

1. Place them in the vacuum-sealable bags and pour into the bags.

2. Prepare sous vide immersion circulator for use according to the manufacturer's directions. Preheat at water to 126°F (52°C).
3. Put the bags in the circulating water then cook it for 30 minutes for medium doneness.
4. Remove the bags from circulating water. Remove the menu from the bags and put them to dry. Taste and adjust the spices.
5. Serve, pancake soup in a bowl and with pomegranate arils, pumpkin seeds, fresh parsley and freshly ground black pepper.
6. Then serve.
7. Cool residues in an airtight container for 4 days

Delicious Fishing Head

Ingredients:

Servings: 4

- 2 TBSP. butter
- 1 big leek, chopped
- 1/2 cup chopped french mussel notes
- Salt
- Dry white wine 3/4 cup

- 1 ¼ cup chicken broth
- 1/2 cup fresh fennel pear, chopped
- 1 kg of small red potatoes
- Season with salt and pepper
- a pinch of cayenne pepper
- 1/2 cup cream 35%
- 1 kg of fish fillets boneless, cut into pieces
- 1 C. chopped fresh tarragon

Preparation time: 20 min

Cooking time: 30 min

Ready in: 50 min

Preparation step:

1. Melt the butter in a saucepan over medium heat and brown leek and scallops with 1/2 teaspoon. Salt, about 10-15 minutes.
2. Put the white wine in the pan; Cook for 2 minutes. Add chicken stock and cook; Add fennel and potatoes and cook until tender. 10 mins
3. Season with salt, pepper and cayenne pepper. Add cream and mix. Dip the pieces of fish with the kite in the liquid. Deck and cook for 3 minutes.
4. Reduce the sous vide vaccum temperature to medium to low heat and cook until the fish peels off with a fork.
5. Season with salt and pepper before serving.

Tuna and Vegetable Salad

Ingredients:

- 2 medium-sized zucchini (thinly cut)
- 2 medium sized carrots (cut in matches)
- 3 cans of tuna (each 5 ounces drained in water)
- 4 sticks of celery (cut and chopped)
- 1 onion (small, thinly sliced)
- 1 tablespoon of fresh, flat parsley (chopped roughly)
- 4 lettuce leaves (iceberg)
- 1/2 cup dressing (light fench)
- 2 tablespoons of yogurt
- 1 garlic clove (crushed)
- 2 teaspoons curry powder

Directions:

1. Cook the zucchini and carrots in a sous vide vaccum. Drain and change to cold water.
2. For the dressing, put all the ingredients in a small bowl and season to taste.
3. Place the zucchini and carrots with tuna, celery, onions, parsley and dressing in a medium bowl and mix gently.

4. Add the salad to the lettuce leaves and serve.

Northern Italian Cattle Head

Preparation: 30 m

Cooking: 4 hours 20 m

Ready for 4 hours 50 m

Ingredients:

- 2 tablespoons olive oil
- 2 pounds of lean buds, cut and cut into 1-inch cubes
- 2 large sweet onions, cubes
- 2 cups of celery
- 4 large carrots, peeled, slice into large circles
- 1 pound Crimini mushrooms, slices
- 2 tablespoons chopped garlic
- 2 cups of dry red wine
- 4 large tomatoes, chopped
- 1 1/2 pounds of red potatoes (like red bliss), cut into 1-inch pieces
- 1 tablespoon of dried basil
- 1 teaspoon dried thyme

- 1 teaspoon dried marjoram
- 1/2 teaspoon dried sage
- 1 quartz beer
- 2 cups tomato sauce

Preparation:

1. Place them in the vacuum-sealable bags and pour into the bags.
2. Prepare sous vide immersion circulator for use according to the manufacturer's directions. Preheat at water to 126°F (52°C).
3. Put the bags in the circulating water then cook it for 30 minutes for medium doneness.
4. Remove the bags from circulating water. Remove the menu from the bags and put them to dry.
5. Put the meat with potatoes, basil, thyme, marjoram and sage in the pan. Pour the beef tomato sauce over the mixture. Bring the liquid to a boil.
6. Reduce the heat to low and cook until the meat is tender and the sauce is 4 to 6 hours thick.

Chicken Soup

Servings: 1 large pot

Ingredients:

- 1 chicken fillet
- 2 chicken thighs
- 5 medium-sized Yukon / yellow potatoes peeled and diced
- 1.5 cups of pasta
- 1 medium carrot
- 1 medium onion cube
- 1 pepper boy
- Chopped parsley
- 1 cup / can of cooked mushrooms
- 1 can be black beans
- Salt
- Black pepper
- 1 garlic clove peeled, pressed

Preparation:

1. Place them in the vacuum-sealable bags and pour into the bags.
2. Prepare sous vide immersion circulator for use according to the manufacturer's directions. Preheat at water to 126°F (52°C).
3. Put the bags in the circulating water then cook it for 30 minutes for medium doneness.
4. Remove the bags from circulating water. Remove the menu from the bags and put them to dry. Serve with a cream.

Chicken Noodle

Ingredients:

- dumplings / pasta
- 1 egg
- 2 tablespoons of vegetables / olive oil
- 3 tablespoons of water
- 1 cup all-purpose flour
- Soup
- 4 qts of water

- 5-6 chicken barrels
- 1 cup of dried mushrooms
- 1 large carrot cut in half
- 1 large onion halved
- 1 teaspoon of black peppercorns
- 1 cup heavy whipped cream
- 1 teaspoon salt
- Serve
- Chopped parsley

Preparation:

1. Place them in the vacuum-sealable bags and pour into the bags.
2. Prepare sous vide immersion circulator for use according to the manufacturer's directions. Preheat at water to 126°F (52°C).
3. Put the bags in the circulating water then cook it for 30 minutes for medium doneness.
4. Remove the bags from circulating water. Remove the menu from the bags and put them to dry.
5. Pull the broth through a fine-mesh sieve and discard the cooked vegetables.
6. Roll the dough as thin as possible. Cut into thin 1-2-inch strips or small squares (1 x 1 inch).
7. Boil the cooking, add the fried vegetables and let the homemade pasta fall into the air. Carefully stir with a spoon. Boil the soup again, add salt and reduce the heat. Cooking for pasta / dumplings are soft, but all dough.
8. Add cream, mushrooms and chicken. Cook again and turn off the heat.
9. Sprinkle with chopped parsley and server.

A Pot Dumble Recipe

Ingredients:

- 2 tablespoons unsalted butter
- 2 tablespoons olive oil
- 2 pound stew or deep-fry (trimmed with fat and cut into 1-inch cubes)
- Finely chop 3 tablespoons of garlic
- Finely chop 1 cup of onion
- 4 medium-sized carrot cubes
- 3 voiced dice
- 1 bay leaf
- 1/3 cup of red wine
- 3 tablespoons of tomato puree
- 1 teaspoon of oregano dried
- 1 teaspoon dried thyme
- 1 teaspoon dried parsley
- salt for the taste
- Pepper For the taste

- 1/2 teaspoon paprika
- 4 cups of low sodium beef stock
- 2 tablespoons all-purpose flour
- 3 medium-sized potato cubes in 1-inch cubes
- 1/2 cup of green beans frozen
- 1/2 cup peas frozen
- 2 tablespoons freshly chopped parsley, garnish

Preparation:

1. Place them in the vacuum-sealable bags and pour into the bags.
2. Prepare sous vide immersion circulator for use according to the manufacturer's directions. Preheat at water to 126°F (52°C).
3. Put the bags in the circulating water then cook it for 30 minutes for medium doneness.
4. Remove the bags from circulating water. Remove the menu from the bags and put them to dry. Garnish with fresh parsley and enjoy.

Bovine Stick

Preparation time: 15 minutes

Cooking time: 35 minutes

Total time: 50 minutes

Ingredients:

- 1 1/2 pounds of beef roast meat

- 1 tablespoon of olive oil

- 1 teaspoon salt

- 1 teaspoon of pepper

- 1 teaspoon of Italian spices

- 2 tablespoons of Worcestershire sauce

- 3 garlic cloves, chopped

- 1 large onion, chopped

- 1 16 ounce sack of carrots, sliced

- 1 pound of potatoes, diced

- 2 1/2 cups of beef broth

- 1 10 oz can be tomato sauce

- 2 tablespoons cornmeal

- 2 tablespoons of water

Preparation

1. Place them in the vacuum-sealable bags and pour into the bags.
2. Prepare sous vide immersion circulator for use according to the manufacturer's directions. Preheat at water to 126°F (52°C).
3. Put the bags in the circulating water then cook it for 30 minutes for medium doneness.
4. Remove the bags from circulating water. Remove the menu from the bags and put them to dry. Mix the cornstarch with cold water inside a small bowl with the stir until thick.

Best Beef Stew

Ingredients:

- 1 tablespoon butter

- 1 pound of cattle feed, cut into 1-inch cubes
- 4 Yukon Gold Potatoes, diced
- 1 1/2 cups of mushrooms, halved
- 1 onion, cut into 6 pieces
- Cut 2 carrots into 1/2 inch thick slices
- 2 garlic cloves, chopped
- 3 cups beef broth
- 1 tablespoon of Worcestershire sauce
- 1 tablespoon of tomato puree
- 1 teaspoon salt
- 1/2 teaspoon ground black pepper
- 1/2 teaspoon dried rosemary

Preparation:

1. Place them in the vacuum-sealable bags and pour into the bags.
2. Prepare sous vide immersion circulator for use according to the manufacturer's directions. Preheat at water to 126°F (52°C).
3. Put the bags in the circulating water then cook it for 30 minutes for medium doneness.
4. Remove the bags from circulating water. Remove the menu from the bags and put them to dry.

Beef and Vegetable Stew

- Ingredients:
- 1 pound low-fat cottage cheese, cut into chisel-shaped pieces
- 2 tablespoons of olive oil or even more, depending on your taste
- 1 large onion, cube
- 3 garlic cloves, finely chopped
- 1 splash of red wine (optional)
- 3 cups of chopped carrots
- 2 cups of chopped celery
- 1 1/2 cups canned checkered tomatoes
- 1 1/2 cups chicken broth
- 1 spiced fresh thyme
- 1 bay leaf and ground black pepper to taste
- 1/3 cup chicken broth
- 2 tablespoons cornmeal

Preparation time: 15 m

Cooking: 1 hour 10 m

Ready in 1 hour 30 m

Preparation:

1. Place them in the vacuum-sealable bags and pour into the bags.
2. Prepare sous vide immersion circulator for use according to the manufacturer's directions. Preheat at water to 126°F (52°C).
3. Put the bags in the circulating water then cook it for 30 minutes for medium doneness.
4. Remove the bags from circulating water. Remove the menu from the bags and put them to dry.

Irish Cattle Head

Ingredients

- 1 1/2 pounds of ground beef
- 1 1/2 teaspoons of garlic salt
- 1/2 teaspoon black pepper
- 2 tablespoons of flour
- 2 tablespoons butter
- 3 garlic cloves, chopped
- 2 cups beef broth
- 2 pounds of reddish-brown potatoes, scrubbed and cut into 1-inch cubes

- 2 medium carrots, roughly chopped
- 1 medium onion, diced
- 1 tablespoon of Worcestershire sauce
- 1 tablespoon of coconut (soy-free spice sauce)
- 2 teaspoons steak sauce
- 1 teaspoon brown sauce
- 1 1/2 teaspoons of dried rosemary
- 1/2 teaspoon dried thyme
- 1 teaspoon of salt or to taste (optional)

Preparation: 15 m

Preparation: 1 hour 5 m

Ready in 1 hour 35 m

Preparation:

1. Place the stew in a large bowl and Season seasonally with garlic salt and pepper. Add flour and butter. Set meat aside.
1. Place them in the vacuum-sealable bags and pour into the bags.
2. Prepare sous vide immersion circulator for use according to the manufacturer's directions. Preheat at water to 126°F (52°C).
3. Put the bags in the circulating water then cook it for 30 minutes for medium doneness.
4. Remove the bags from circulating water. Remove the menu from the bags and put them to dry.
5. Add Worcestershire sauce, coconut-Aminos, steak sauce, tanning sauce, rosemary and thyme to the pool and stir to mix. If necessary, season to taste and season with salt.

Nutritional information:

- 409 calories
- 19.6 g fat
- 34.5 g of carbohydrate

- 23.3 g protein
- 73 mg cholesterol
- 1298 mg of sodium

Beef And Vegetable Soup

Ingredients:

- 1 tablespoon of olive oil
- 2 pounds of boneless skewers, diced or seasoned
- 5 big carrots, chopped
- 1 large yellow onion, chopped
- 2 celery stalks, 6 cups of water chopped
- 3 large robes, peeled and diced
- 1 pound of fresh green beans, cut and cut
- 2 tablespoons of tomatoes
- 2 tablespoons salt or more to taste
- 2 tablespoons of garlic powder or more to taste
- 1 tablespoon of onion powder or more to taste
- 1 tablespoon of celery seed
- 2 bay leaves leaves of black pepper to taste

Preparation: 30 m

Kitchen: 50 m

Ready in 1 hour 30 m

Preparation:

2. Place them in the vacuum-sealable bags and pour into the bags.
3. Prepare sous vide immersion circulator for use according to the manufacturer's directions. Preheat at water to 126°F (52°C).
4. Put the bags in the circulating water then cook it for 30 minutes for medium doneness.
5. Remove the bags from circulating water. Remove the menu from the bags and put them to dry.

Medicined Meat With Frozen Meat

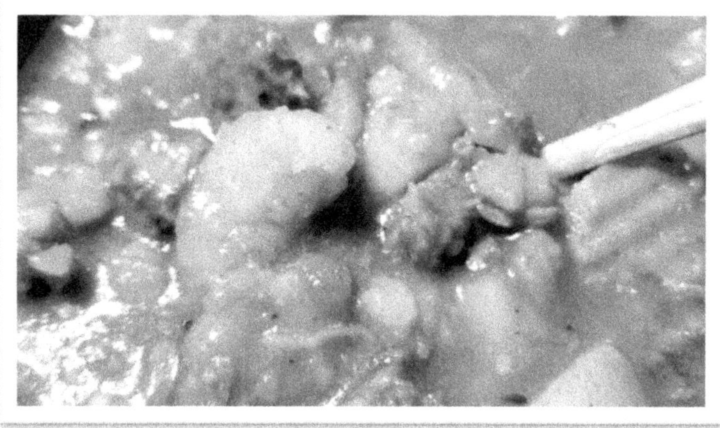

Preparation: 20 m

Cooking: 1 hour 25 m

Done in: 1 hour 45 m

Ingredients:

- 1 tablespoon of avocado oil
- 1 large onion, fine cake

- 3 garlic cloves, finely chopped
- 1/4 cup of dry red wine
- 2 cups beef broth
- 1 teaspoon of thyme
- 1 teaspoon dried parsley
- 1 teaspoon dried oregano
- 1 sheet of paper
- 1 teaspoon of salt or to taste
- 1/2 teaspoon ground black pepper
- 1 tablespoon of tomato puree
- Beef pies with 2 (1 pound) pack, frozen
- 5 large baked potatoes, peeled and sliced
- 3/4 inch pieces of 6 medium carrots, slices
- 3 celery ribs, sliced
- 2 tablespoons of water
- 1 tablespoon cornmeal

Preparation:

1. Place them in the vacuum-sealable bags and pour into the bags.
2. Prepare sous vide immersion circulator for use according to the manufacturer's directions. Preheat at water to 126°F (52°C).
3. Put the bags in the circulating water then cook it for 30 minutes for medium doneness.
4. Remove the bags from circulating water. Remove the menu from the bags and put them to dry.

Bovine Stick

Preparation time: 15 minutes

Preparation time: 35 minutes

Total time: 50 minutes

Ingredients:

- 1 1/2 pounds of beef stew
- 1 tablespoon of olive oil
- 1 teaspoon salt
- 1 teaspoon of pepper
- 1 teaspoon Italian herbs
- 2 tablespoons of Worcestershire sauce
- 3 garlic cloves, chopped
- 1 large onion, chopped
- 1 16 bags of baby carrots, cut
- 1 pound of potatoes in cubes
- 2 1/2 cups of beef broth
- 1-2 tomato sauce
- 2 tablespoons cornmeal
- 2 tablespoons of water

Instructions:

1. Place them in the vacuum-sealable bags and pour into the bags.
2. Prepare sous vide immersion circulator for use according to the manufacturer's directions. Preheat at water to 126°F (52°C).
3. Put the bags in the circulating water then cook it for 30 minutes for medium doneness.
4. Remove the bags from circulating water. Remove the menu from the bags and put them to dry.
5. Mix flour and cold water in a small bowl and stir in the stew until thicker.

Nutrition:

- Calories: 384 kcal

- Carbohydrates: 23 g

Protein: 42 g

- Fat: 12 g

- Saturated fat: 3 g

- Cholesterol: 105 mg

- Sodium: 1333 mg

- Potassium: 1246 mg

- Fiber: 3 g

- Sugar: 2 g

- Vitamin A: 0.7%

- Vitamin C: 20.3%

Calcium: 10.3%

- Iron: 45.4%

Bovine Heart

Preparation time 20 minutes

Cooking time 4 hours

Total time 4 hours and 20 minutes

Ingredients

- 2 tablespoons olive oil
- 2 pounds of stew
- Salt and pepper to taste
- 2 tablespoons all-purpose flour
- 1 teaspoon dried thyme
- 2 teaspoons of smoked paprika
- 1 large onion, cube
- 3 garlic cloves, pressed
- 3 medium carrots, chopped
- 2 celery stalks, chopped

- 1/2 cup of red wine
- 2 strips of Worcestershire sauce
- 2 tablespoons of tomato puree
- 1/2 cup tomato sauce
- 3 cups low sodium beef
- 5 medium white potatoes, quartered
- 1 cup of frozen green beans (optional)
- fresh parsley for garnish

Instructions:

1. Prepare the sous vide vaccum.
2. Sprinkle meat with salt and pepper with place in the sous vide vaccum.
3. Roast the pieces of meat on each side until they are nicely caramelized, and sprinkle the flour over the meat when it is brown, about 1 teaspoon at a time.
4. Take the meat out of the sous vide vaccum on a plate after it has turned brown (do not worry now!) And add thyme, smoked paprika, onion, garlic, carrots and celery to the pot.
5. Stir vegetables around to catch all the drops in the meat jar and put the beef back in the jar after the onions are almost translucent.
6. Add red wine, Worcestershire sauce and tomato purée. Stir well and let the liquid cool (it is important to boil the wine for 4-5 minutes before adding the other liquid).
7. When the wine liqueur has thickened and thickened for a few minutes, add the tomato sauce, the beef broth and the potatoes.
8. Give everything a good feel, scrape off all parts from the bottom of the pot.
9. Make sure the potatoes are well embedded in the liquid and add the lid to the pot. Put in the sous vide vaccum Fahrenheit for about 3 to 3.5 hours.

10. Remove the lid from the pan every few hours and let it stir quickly.
11. If you want to add frozen green beans (these are optional and I only add about 50% of the cooking time), stir them in the last 30 minutes so they do not get wet.
12. You know that the stew is ready at the end of the set time and the pieces of meat disintegrate when you touch them with a fork.
13. Serve in deep bowls, add a piece of crispy bread and sprinkle with fresh parsley (if desired).

Mexican Break With Chicken

This Mexican stew is filled with soft chicken pieces, kidney beans, tomatoes, onions and garlic. The whole delicacy is mixed with rice and topped with fresh spring onions and creamy avocado.

Ingredients or 4 people:

- •1 onion
- 1 clove of garlic
- 2 tablespoons of oil
- 600 grams of chicken
- 1 red pepper
- 2 dl of rice
- 4 cups chicken broth

- 1 kidney beans
- 1 chopped tomato
- possibly 2 cups of corn
- 1 teaspoon of cumin
- possible. 1 teaspoon of chilli powder
- Salt
- Pepper
- to cover it
- 4 tomatoes
- 1 night spring onion
- 2 avocados
- a bit of lime juice or lemon juice
- 100 grams of grated cheddar cheese
- sour cream

Preparation:

1. Finely chop the onion and garlic. Soak in a pan in the oil.
2. Cut the chicken into a slice and place in the pan. Stir well so they can be changed from all sides.
3. Slice the pepper into small cubes and add to the pan with rice. Let it cook for half a minute while stirring.
4. Add the chicken stock. Pour the alcohol from the kidney beans and put them together with the chopped tomatoes and possibly in the pan. May add the caraway and possibly. chili
5. Leave the bowl for about 15 minutes or until the rice is ready.
6. In the meantime the refilling is finished. Cut the tomatoes in half, remove soft grains and cut "tomato meat" into small cubes. Finely chop the spring onions.
7. Cut the avocados lengthwise, remove the stones and remove the green pulp with a spoon. Add cubes and lime juice or lemon juice.

8. Taste the dish with salt and pepper and serve it with the topping.

African stew

It's not often that you meet African recipes, but this stew is really worth trying. Beef, onions and tomatoes give a beautiful texture and the many herbs give the dish a full flavor.

Ingredients for 4 people:

- 2 red onions
- 5 tomatoes
- A little oil
- 3 garlic cloves
- 400 g duck leg
- 1/2 teaspoon with clove
- 1 1 teaspoon of cardamom
- 2 teaspoons of caraway
- 3/4 teaspoon cinnamon
- 1 teaspoon of pepper
- 3 dl basmati rice
- Water (depending on the package)
- 1 block beef broth
- possible. salt

- Equipment
- 1 red onion
- Water
- 1 tablespoon salt
- 2 tomatoes
- possible. fresh coriander

Preparation

1. Finely chop red onions and tomatoes. Vacuum-sealable bags. Press garlic and add it.

2. Cut the meat into a slice and add it with cloves, cardamom, cumin, cinnamon and pepper. Cook until the meat is tender and then add the rice. Fry them a little and then add the amount of water you want to use (depending on the package). Also add the beef stock and let the bowl cook. Then turn the low heat over and cook the bowl for about 10-15 minutes or until the rice is tender.

3. Taste everything. Add some salt, but keep it a little, because the accessories are also salty.

Domestic equipments:

• Cut the onion into thin slices and place in a bowl. Cover with water and add salt to the water. Let it soak for 10 minutes. Rinse the onion slices under running cold water and place in a bowl.

• Cut the tomatoes into thin slices and tear them apart. Take them with the onions in the bowl and mix them together. Serve it as an accessory for the African stew - possibly. With some fresh coriander.

Chili con carne

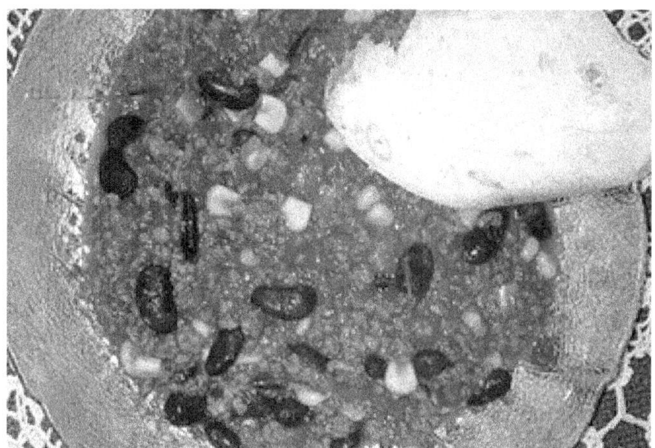

Ingredients:

- 1 kg   ground beef
- 800g   Kidney beans, washed and drained
- 400g   Corn, canned, drained
- 800g   Tomato (s), lumpy
- 1 big one   Onion (s), diced
- 200 ml   tomato juice
- 2 tbsp   chili powder
- salt and pepper
- 1 teaspoon   Oregano or mexican oregano
- 150 ml   Water or broth
- 2 tbsp   rapeseed oil.

Working time: approx. 30 min

Preparation:

1. Fry the onions and minced meat with 1 tablespoon of chili, salt and pepper in Saute or More stage in the instant pot.
2. Deglaze with the tomato juice and let reduce. Add beans, corn, tomatoes and oregano vacuum-sealable bags and add the stock while stirring. Put on the lid of the vacuum-

sealable bags and cook for 7 minutes at Steam or High Pressure and season with the remaining chilli if necessary.

3. The chili is generally served only with bread.

Tip: Due to the previous sautéing, the pot needs about 5 minutes to build up pressure and another 7 minutes to cook.

Potato and corn curry

Ingredients:

- 1 kg   Potato (s), approx. 5
- 450 g   Corn
- 3   Garlic clove (s), chopped
- 1 Pepper (s), red, cut small
- 1 Onion (s), chopped
- 2 Tea spoons   Paprika powder, smoked
- 260 ml   vegetable stock
- 400 ml   coconut milk
- salt

Working time: approx. 25 min

Preparation:

1. Place them in the vacuum-sealable bags and pour into the bags.

2. Prepare sous vide immersion circulator for use according to the manufacturer's directions. Preheat the water to 126°F (52°C).
3. Put the bags in the circulating water and then cook for 30 minutes for medium doneness.
4. Remove the bags from the circulating water. Remove the menu from the bags and put them to dry.

Pea rice in instant pot

Ingredients:

- 1 cup   Brown rice, z. B. Basmati, round grain or wild rice
- 1 cup   water
- 1 cup   Peas, TK
- vegetable stock
- pepper
- garlic powder
- turmeric
- Salt or soy sauce (shoyu)
- Working time: approx. 2 minutes
- cooking time: approx. 22 minutes

Preparation:

1. Cook the brown rice with the water and spices for 20 minutes in the manual program. Then add the frozen peas, maybe add water and cook for 2 minutes in the manual program.
2. If necessary, season again and add salt or soy sauce to the plate.

Vegetable Salad With Ricotta

Ingredients:

- 1 bunch of baby beets
- 1 bunch baby carrots (cleaned and trimmed)
- 1 bunch of asparagus (cut at the end)
- 4 ounces of green beans (trimmed)
- 4 ounces of mangetout (trimmed)
- 1 1/2 cups ricotta cheese
- 1 tablespoons of chives (finely chopped)
- 1 tablespoons lemon juice
- 1 tablespoon extra virgin olive oil
- 1 tablespoon balsamic vinegar

Preparation:

1. Cut the turnips off and leave 1 inch stems. Wash the skin thoroughly. Put inside a pan and cover with cold water. Bring to a boil. Cook for 10 minutes or until done. Pump, cool, peel and halve. Boil the remaining vegetables in a pan of boiling water for 2 to 5 minutes until tender and still crispy. Drain and cool.
2. Beat the ricotta with a fork until light and fluffy. Stir in the chives and lemon juice and season with the season. Bunch of ricotta in the middle of the trays. Arrange vegetables around ricotta. Sprinkle vegetables with 1 tablespoon of lemon juice, sprinkle with oil and balsamic vinegar and serve.